MW01282210

My Journey Through Homelessness

Homelessness

The Real Story

Written by

STIGMATIZED HEARTS

ISBN: 978-1-4969-5265-3 (sc)
ISBN: 978-1-4969-5386-5 (e)

This book is printed on acid-free paper.

Because of the dynamic nature of the Internet, any web addresses or
links contained in this book may have changed since publication and
may no longer be valid. The views expressed in this work are solely those
of the author and do not necessarily reflect the views of the publisher,
and the publisher hereby disclaims any responsibility for them.

Preface

This book is the product of a project undertaken by graduate students in a social work program located in a large city in the southwest. It is a collaborative effort between the students; an organization that provides a range of services aimed at improving the lives of people with mental health disorders, substance use challenges, and disabilities; and a residential community of individuals who are homeless. The stories, poems, and artwork in this book share the unique stories of men and women participating in a comprehensive wellness program.

As represented through the stories in this book, mental illness and substance use are common among experiencing homelessness. These issues present a formidable challenge to anyone attempting to rise out of homelessness. Nearly one in three individuals who experience long-term homelessness has a mental health condition; one in two members of this group has a co-occurring substance use problem.

The authors of this book came to the residential community in which they currently live under vastly different circumstances. The stories that follow include those of veterans, suburban mothers, recently arrived immigrants, individuals with college degrees, the son of Holocaust survivors, and many more. Each of them has experienced some form of serious trauma such as serious physical or sexual assault, witnessing severe injury or death, being involved in a life-threatening accident, or having combat experience in a war zone. This book is designed to share the stories of these individuals, portraying the *real people*, rather than simply the homelessness with which they have been labeled. These stories demonstrate with conviction that homelessness is a *condition*, not a choice.

What we have learned is that for the most part, becoming homeless does not occur suddenly, but is most often associated with a downward spiral that begins with a significant negative life event or a series of such events from which the individual is unable to recover. How quickly individuals traverse the spiral depends on the resources upon which they can draw, such as financial savings or friends and family members who are willing to take them in.

Downward Spiral of Homelessness

Lose job/regular financial support

↓

Exhaust savings

↓

Move-in with friend/family member

↓

Live out of car

↓

Live on the streets

As students participating in this project, we had the privilege of spending time with the authors of this book over the course of three months, learning about their life stories as well as their hopes and dreams for the future. We were honored to share time, food, and emotional moments with these individuals, who have spent a significant part of their lives living at the margins of society. We learned about them as well as *from* them. Our lives were forever changed by the experience.

The feelings of several class members about their participation in the project are captured by the following quotes:

"This project brought an overwhelming feeling of emotions for me … I realized that the members here are only trying to survive …"

"The power of human connection was truly evident through the experience in working with these individuals … Their ability to find purpose through triumph led to one takeaway: we all have a social responsibility as humans to see each other as equals …"

"As a future social worker, I was excited about the prospect of 'helping' homeless individuals by spending time with them and hearing their stories … Every story of tough circumstances, heartbreaking beginnings, poor choices, and mental health issues beyond their control … was my lesson to learn."

"They have no idea as to how their stories have helped me; their willingness to share their experiences to the world has given me so much hope as a future social worker."

"The thing that most amazed me … was how willing they were to open themselves up to a world that consistently ignores and stigmatizes them. Their willingness to be vulnerable in sharing their story … was moving beyond words."

It is our hope that by reading this book, you will come to appreciate the challenges that people who are homeless and have a co-occurring mental health and substance use disorder face on a daily basis and the impact of these challenges on the individuals' ability to secure and keep a job, find affordable housing, and live independently (without financial or other assistance). It is also our hope that you will come to admire the unique strengths and resilience that characterize these individuals. Our final hope is that you will stand up and take action to do your part to end homelessness - in your back yard, in your community, and in society.

Introduction

"True compassion is more than flinging a coin to a beggar; it understands that an edifice which produces beggars needs restructuring"

Martin Luther King Jr.

Homelessness is the great American tragedy. Many of us are uncomfortable when we encounter an individual who is homeless. The stereotypes of persons experiencing homelessness reflexively come to mind: the individual could be dangerous and become aggressive; s(he) might be bearing an infectious disease; giving the individual money will only lead to the purchase of alcohol and drugs; or the individual appears to be able-bodied and is too lazy to get a job. Some people go out of their way to avoid such an encounter with an individual who is homeless by either crossing the street, rushing by the individual without acknowledging her or him in some way, or waiting until the individual moves on.

> A person is considered homeless who lacks a fixed, regular, and adequate night-time residence; and... has a primary night time residency that is: (A) a supervised publicly or privately operated shelter designed to provide temporary living accommodations... (B) an institution that provides a temporary residence for individuals intended to be institutionalized, or (C) a public or private place not designed for, or ordinarily used as, a regular sleeping accommodation for human beings. [Stewart B. McKinney Act, 42 U.S.C. § 11301, et seq. (1994)]

As many as 3.5 million people in the U.S. experience homelessness in a given year - 1% of the entire U.S. population - 1 in 10 of the country's poor. Primary causes of homelessness include poverty, eroding work opportunities, a decline in public assistance, lack of affordable housing (including foreclosure due to mortgage default), and interpersonal violence and other trauma. Secondary causes of homelessness include lack of affordable health care, mental illness, addiction disorders, and release from incarceration.

Being homeless and having an untreated mental health and/or substance use disorder make it extremely difficult for a person to return to mainstream society. The quality of life for such individuals can at best be characterized as abysmal. Many of them have spent the majority of their lives living on the streets, in some type of mental health facility, in and out of jail, or in homeless shelters.

There is a direct link between poor mental health and physical health. Persons with untreated mental health problems frequently engage in high-risk behaviors that can lead to diseases such as hepatitis, tuberculosis, HIV or AIDS. Inadequate hygiene and exposure to weather extremes are commonly associated with a variety of skin and other diseases among individuals who have been living on the streets for a long time.

There is a strong relationship between alcohol and drug use and homelessness, especially among those with untreated mental health issues who may attempt to self-medicate to deal with their illness or to deaden the pain of present and past life experiences. Many individuals become homeless because of the debilitating effects of long-term alcohol or drug addiction. Some mentally ill people self-medicate with street drugs, with heroin the most common because of its ready availability and relatively low cost. Opiate dependence is one of the most difficult forms of drug use to treat and manage and is associated with a plethora of health problems such as respiratory illness, heart disease, kidney disease, and liver disease.

The number of people who are homeless with serious untreated mental illness has been steadily increasing since the deinstitutionalization movement that began in the 1970s. This trend does not bode well for the future either. There is a strong correlation between discharge from a mental health facility and an increase in crime, arrest rates, and homelessness. The promise of care in community-based settings for individuals experiencing mental health problems has never materialized. Getting an appointment in a community-based mental health clinic often takes months to obtain. Drugs prescribed for people who are homeless with severe mental illness are often misused, lost, or stolen. Many individuals who are homeless resist taking medications prescribed for them because of the side effects they cause.

It is not uncommon for individuals who are homeless and have been on the street for a long time, to have experienced some form of extreme trauma such as physical or sexual assault, witnessing death, or incarceration. Often, these traumas, such as traumatic brain injury (TBI) or Post-traumatic Stress Disorder (PTSD), are invisible to the naked eye. Increasingly, programs for the homeless are adopting trauma-informed interventions; however, this practice is relatively new and the long-term efficacy of such interventions has yet to be determined.

Housing first or rapid-rehousing initiatives are also on the rise among programs serving individuals experiencing homelessness as there is a clear relationship between the time a person spends on the streets and long-term homelessness. To be successful, such initiatives need to be coupled with ongoing community-based care, especially for those individuals with severe mental health problems. Recidivism rates for individuals who are homeless and are part of rapid re-housing initiatives are especially high when such community-based care and supports are sporadic or nonexistent.

The individuals whose stories appear in this book represent a microcosm of the problems raised above. They are viewed by many as castaways from a society that has limited safety net programs and a general lack of concern for those who do not fit the so-called "American ideal".

Their plight will continue, and even worsen, unless we make a significant investment in preventing homelessness from occurring in the first place and providing adequate and consistent services for those currently sharing this experience.

In spite of their plight, the men and women who generously shared their life stories for this project show tremendous strength, resilience, and courage in overcoming their condition.

Acknowledgements

Twenty-nine students worked tirelessly over a three-month period to complete this book. The unique contribution of each of these students is acknowledged here. Their ethnographic interviewing skills and compassion played a significant role in eliciting the stories contained herein. Their ability to work with little direct supervision was nothing short of amazing. Their persistence in securing cash and in-kind donations on behalf of the project made it possible for the project to be completed on time and within budget. Completion of this book is a legacy to their accomplishments.

Completion of this project would not have been possible without the leadership and support of the administrator of the wellness program from which the authors of this book were drawn and her staff and the staff of the residential facility in which the authors lived.

We would also like to acknowledge the generous donations made to the project by several individuals and businesses located in the city in which the project was conducted.

Lastly, a very special thank you goes to the authors and artists who contributed to this project. Their willingness to share their life stories and their indomitable spirit has reaffirmed our passion and commitment to the social work profession. All names and identifying details have been changed to protect the privacy of these individuals.

My Journey Through Homelessness

The Real Story

Popeye

*"A simple hi, someone to acknowledge my existence
has helped me get through life."*

I have been on the streets the majority of my life, about
30 years now. It is not constant. Some of it was out of choice,
but most of it wasn't.

I have no family. Except one sister and maybe a brother,
I'm not sure. I have heard about him, but I have never seen
him. I'm originally from the West, moved to the South for
my mom. At 13, I was living in a tent in the Southwest,
where my uncle was the mayor. No one really bothered me,
but I'm sure my uncle had people watching out for me. I
was able to graduate high school and eventually ended up
in another city in the Southwest.

From there I made it to the South. My mom called
me from work saying some guy was hitting her so I started
walking to where she was. I got a ride for the first 30 miles,

but I walked the rest of the way. I was on a mission. I tried to stop at bridges to catch a ride and walked right through any towns so I wouldn't be stopped by police. It took me 3 days and I barely slept because of the noise and dangers on the road. When I finally saw my mom she said, "He's not here, he's not here." As soon as we hung up the phone he left. I'm sure he was scared knowing I was coming with my gun in hand. It was probably a good thing he wasn't there when I showed up. I was going to shoot him.

I hear everything. I was born with only 60% use in my ear. But everything sounds loud. I have to sleep with earplugs when I sleep outside and I still hear everything. I wake up very easily. I do not have a problem surviving. I am able to adapt and survive. I've gone from living in a tent, to having a job and all the good stuff. I used to live the "Rock n' Roll' lifestyle. There were no limitations, no rules. I did what I wanted to do. Four to five years ago, any ordinary persons would have not approached me. I was intimidating, hair all over my face.

I have few people that I can actually call friends. If I were to call them for a place to go, they would be there, no question about it. Relationships are very important to me. Sometimes I just need to be acknowledged. I once was stopped from jumping off the bridge because a stranger walked by and told me, "Hi." I didn't want to live anymore and someone came by and just said, "Hi." That's all I needed as motivation to turn around and say it wasn't worth it to end my life. I've gotten close to death several times, I've been in the intensive care unit seven times; life is hard to deal with. It has led me to drink bottles of alcohol and try to walk in front of a train to get away from my past and all the bad things I've dealt with. But in the end, something always stops me.

My mother died in my arms in 2006. The last words she ever said to me were, "Don't forget to breathe." This has caused a lot of my anger. On her birthday, I do not do so well. It has gotten better, but I struggle. I have walked in front of a moving train with a bottle of whisky in my hand on her birthday. That is the toughest day for me right now.

Many people see me differently. For example, the law stereotypes me as homeless and that automatically gets you into trouble. I have had to deal with a lot of people. One time, I asked a woman for directions. I had a beard covering my face. When she looked up to see me, she dropped her purse and ran in the opposite direction. I was not trying to scare her, I just wanted directions. But that is how people treat you sometimes. Society treats us differently. They strip us of our human dignity with how they treat us. We are shunned for how we look, talk, and dress. It is like we are forced to fit a stereotype. You would think that people would understand that, as a human species, no one wants to be judged at the end of the day.

Not everyone is bad. I have learned over the years how to survive. I have met people who have helped me along the way. Survival has taught me how to bargain with people. For example, I used to sleep on the porch of a lawyer's office. I figured I'd do the right thing and ask him if it would be okay if I slept there, and in return I'd watch over the office and call the authorities if anyone tried to break-in. I let him know he would never see me. I would get there once he is gone for the day and be gone by the time he shows up for work. I would keep the place clean and he'd never know I was there. He agreed and never saw me again. He understood my position and that is why he let me stay. I was able to bargain with him. In exchange for secure shelter, I provided security and kept the place clean. There are a lot of good people out there. They are just hard to come by. I have had people buy me fast food, treated me to lunch, and taken me to the hospital. Without those good experiences who knows where I would be today. It gives me the hope that I am able to think about the people who have genuinely helped me. It changes my perspective on society.

I am just happy to be alive. All the negative things in my past started when I was a child. I have not had a Thanksgiving dinner since the age of 12 or a Christmas dinner in 35 years. I would like to get all those things back, even though sometimes I feel those dreams are gone. I am 43 and it feels like college is out of the question; who would want to hire someone in their 60's? My ultimate goal is not to be homeless. I want to come back to what is familiar, but right now it seems like familiar is waking up to the sounds of the train tracks and the morning sun. I am not sure if it's a mental illness or my anger that I cannot control. I want to live and die in peace.

In my future, I hope to see a white picket fence and a job. I do not take back what I have done in my life. I may not be book smart, and I may not even make it through a book, but I have learned a lot of skills on the streets which have made me smart at what I know. I have managed to stay out of jail, which is a hard thing to do when you're homeless.

The program at the shelter has really helped me. You are a product of your environment. This is a good environment. I have been here for about 5 months and I have the hope that one day I will be back and living on my own, recreating the traditions of Thanksgiving and Christmas I once had.

Matt

*"I would like the opportunity to own my own place
and call something mine."*

I spent the majority of my childhood moving around from place to place. Honestly, it was difficult trying to make friends and find stability. I was born in the West and moved overseas for 3 years. I was very into the culture there and appreciated the beauty. From there, both my mother and I moved to the Southeast, where my sister was born. My mom was in the military, so traveling became part of our everyday routine.

Once we arrived in the Southeast, I was in culture shock. I couldn't believe how different it was than from living overseas, but I got used to moving quick and mostly kept to myself. My sister and I have different fathers, so neither of us has the same last name. My mom was a single mom. It was hard on us financially and emotionally, and it stressed me out. I would get stuck having to watch my sister when my mom wasn't able to – that got old pretty fast. I was the only father figure my sister had, and I would get into arguments with my mom about it. It wasn't fair and I feel bad, because partially I didn't truly understand what exactly taking the father figure role meant, let alone I had my own troubles to deal with. I was angry and depressed. I had a hard time getting along with other kids in my school, and my mother assumed that once I graduated I would end up joining the armed forces like her. I almost joined back in the West, that's just it.

I was in my early twenties, and at that time, everyone in my family was either in the military or a veteran. I wanted to follow in their footsteps and to this day, I never found out why I wasn't accepted. I guess medical reasons? I don't know, maybe I wasn't tough enough. I knew growing up that I had a lot of emotional problems, within the family and the nonstop bullying in school; it got to me. One thing in particular I remember is my stepdad taking my sister out for the day without me. I was 7 years old, and I can remember stepping out and when I returned they were gone. I never found out if it was on purpose, but he was the only father figure I looked up to, and he left me.

I was 27 when I first became homeless. I was living out of my truck, jumping from roommate to roommate, balancing job after job. I suffered from anger and depression issues. At the time I was working at a department store and not coping well. My managers would call me a loser and finally I walked out of the job because I could not take it anymore. I was getting paid 14 dollars an hour, but the pain wasn't worth it. I was being tormented. I attempted to collect recyclables and start a recycling business because in the West there are a lot of recycling centers. "Maybe I would get enough for gas and food," I thought. I didn't want to seem desperate. I refused to be that guy standing out with a sign in the street that pleads, "Please help." During this time, my stickers were expired, and I was towed in a parking lot of a coffee shop. I went inside to ask for help and the employees called the cops on me and told them I was doing meth. Of course, it is illegal to live out of a truck, so the cops took me to jail. Once I was released, I looked for a shelter, or someplace to at least find help. The shelter had several programs there and one helped with Section VIII housing. I became somewhat successful in the program, but resorted back to my anger and depression. Looking back, the classes were nowhere as near comprehensive or intense as the anger management classes at this shelter, and I was not improving. I got kicked out twice, and the first time was that I was not thinking clearly and brought a folding knife and forgot I wasn't allowed to bring it in. The second time, I got into a fight. Somebody came in drunk and I finally had it with them. I resorted to a day shelter. I liked the library there. There's an ongoing joke, homeless people have that. We all like staying in libraries. Well, it's true because it's cold and quiet; something quite rare in my world. But most of all, there is no stereotype. The library was quiet and there was not a lot of people around, I didn't feel judged.

I was 35 years old before I would get the chance to see my mother again. I was living in and out of homelessness and eventually moved back to the South; however, our relationship changed. I would do the chores that she asked me to do, but it still was not good enough. I felt like I was

8 years old again being told I was a failure and was sick of getting yelled at. During this time, I did have a job at a restaurant, bussing tables and washing dishes. I was doing pretty well handling my depression and anger, but I think at this time it was because I was able to keep myself busy. Since then, I moved out and went from roommate to roommate. It's funny how many people you know and how many will let you stay when you have no place to go. But my health was decreasing. I suffered from a lot of anxiety attacks and could not afford treatment. Looking back, I wish I had the confidence to stand up for myself, not only in my childhood but to my mother as well. I should have been accepted into the military. Growing up, I was looking out for my sister and at times even my mother, although I resented her for it.

I've come to realize that it doesn't matter what social class you are from – anyone can be homeless. I had a pretty decent childhood, in the sense that I had food on the table and a bed to sleep in. Anyone has the capacity to become physically or mentally ill and financially struggle. I am not lazy. I work very hard every day and am finally getting the help I have been searching for. I want people to know that I managed to dodge a bullet. You meet a lot of homeless people who sleep under bridges and scrape through the garbage for food; I was lucky that was not me. I held down jobs and was thankful I had a shower. I will forever struggle with my mental health as I am unsure of how long it will take to heal. It may never heal, but I am aware that depression and anger have been the roots to my problem. I want to find a career and restart my life. If I had the opportunity to rewind, I would start a whole new tape! My first goal would be going back to school, though I worry if someone would even hire someone as old as myself.

People ask me a lot, what do I want out of life? I sit here and think to myself, if I could wish for something, it would be a place to call my own. I know that sounds simple but I have never had my own place. I would like the opportunity to own my own place and call something mine. I don't want to remain homeless and trapped, and I have to keep my focus on my recovery from depression in order to succeed within this program. I am not a weak link. I am a survivor.

Samantha

"I wasn't expecting to become homeless."

I was born in the South. We were poor, sometimes we got a break. My parents got rich, got poor - got rich because my daddy sued this construction company. He got hurt by a machine that fell on his leg and broke it. I moved to another city in the South in 1968 when I got married. My divorced husband is from here and his family's here. So we moved here. When we had children in '71, my ex-husband didn't want to raise our children in the city so we moved to the country. That's where we were living for a long time. We finally got divorced. Then I wound up back in the city.

Some memorable childhood experiences, though we were poor most of the time, involved going to church. We were Catholic and they would make us go to church… to those classes, catechism classes… a lot of that. We had a lot of family outings, a lot of dancing.

There were 6 of us, five girls and a boy. My youngest sister died three years ago, so now there are four girls and a boy. They are living further south.

I enjoy listening to the radio and watching TV. I used to listen a lot to the radio but now I am trying to cut back. I like to watch TV but I'm trying to cut back on that too because I am staying here. We have a schedule and we have classes, groups, and we meet with our clinician.

I am trying to go back on my own because I had a boyfriend when I was sleeping outside the shelter. I ended up in the shelter program because I have a lot of medical problems. I would like to try to find myself a place to live, no boyfriends.

I ended up in homelessness when I was working on getting my divorce. My ex-husband was rough on me. I was tired of him abusing us. He almost killed my daughter. He was very violent. He would tell my daughter to get a job and my son to find an apartment. They had just graduated and he wanted to throw them out of the house already.

My ex-husband was abusive while my kids were growing up. He was abusive towards all of us. He was having an affair and I found out, but like I said he was trying to convince the court he wouldn't hurt a fly. So I convinced the court not to believe him because it was his fault that we were getting a divorce. They did overturn some of the things that he was trying to say. And they said no that he cannot have the community property because it belonged to the marriage, but anyway I said all that should have been put in the court how he treated us. Well, he didn't want me to finish high school, he just wanted me there being a housewife taking care of the kids.

He was much older than me when I met him out west. I think I was fourteen when we met. We got married, he was rough. He was so rough. He went to college, he was in the military. He worked for an airport company and he was the one that had the money. He was the one that was supposed to be taking care of me.

I divorced my husband. Individuals at a shelter and university were helping me make plans to get my disability (benefits). I had a divorce lawyer from Legal Aid. The judge was going to decide if I was going to get spousal support. I was going to have to go to court to get my disability to see if I qualified because of my medical problems that I had. I did get some money from my divorce. I still get my spousal support. I had to go to the court to get my money for my disability and they gave me one of those tests, too - a psychological exam.

I had a boyfriend I met at a shelter. He also gave me a rough time. I would try to help out. I would go into a house, try to help out a little bit but he kept on complaining and try to take money out of my bag. He kept saying he wouldn't do it again but finally he said I was old already and he was going to go to a different city. He said, "I'm still married anyways and I am going to go be with my wife over there because she is still young."

He was abusive to me, too. We kept moving around and we could never stay at one place. My boyfriend would try to help poor people with his money but then he expected me to help them, too. I couldn't do that- I had my own problems. I had to pay for myself so we could get a place to live.

My daughter wanted me to live with her, but they needed to get their house repaired, and I didn't want to be a bother.

So I would be sleeping outside the shelter and my boyfriend would get an apartment, but then we would have to relocate.

The last time I saw him was in May, after I was in a program and he went out on his own.

My experience of homelessness has been kind of rough. I wasn't expecting to become homeless. Well at least they gave me a bed at a shelter. Different types of religious people come see us and at the holidays they try to keep us cheerful. That keeps me from thinking of being unhappy. And I get a disability check. I'm not working because I'm disabled.

Mental health has not been the only problem that has played a role in my becoming homeless. I am a diabetic, I have high blood pressure, and some other medical problems. I was also in a car crash. I get so sick. Years ago I got very sick. I had a bladder infection, my stomach was infected. You name it I had it. I was in a nursing home then; they sent me here.

I don't want to be homeless.

But it's not just being homeless. Even shelters get very cold sometimes. They try to get everyone inside when it rains or when it gets cold. But once there was an old man that didn't make it in and he died because it was cold. I didn't know him.

Nowadays they don't want anyone sleeping in downtown areas. They try and give you warnings or they will take you to jail… they don't want us there.

My hope and dream is to find my own place and be on my own again. I don't want to be a homeless person my whole life. I want to make sure I am well enough to be on my own, to live alone, go back to society, and being able to maintain my apartment and keep it clean. I want to get better and healthy.

Untitled

By Matt

No matter how nightmarish yesterday was,
We always awaken into the present,
Creating an ever growing past with
all the solidity of a dream.

What dream would you like to awaken from?

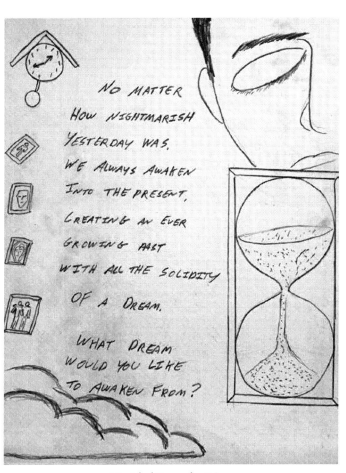

Untitled Poem by Matt

Randy

"It's like a trap. I'm in it. I'm in a maze and I can't find my way out."

I grew up in a large city in the South in a family of 12. I dropped out of school at the age of 13, and started getting into trouble. I committed a crime and even though it was my first offense, I received a 5 year sentence. My dad was thinking about buying a house, but he never got to that point. We just rented. My dad did seasonal work and sometimes we would have to go to the church and have to ask for money or food.

I served 2 years and 8 months of my sentence. When I got out of prison I learned how to be a Christian so I could change my ways instead of living that criminal life. I stayed there for 5 years. It was more or less like a shelter or a halfway house. My experience there was good. Most of it was based on Christianity. I went there because I wanted to know how to live the Christian life. They told me about Jesus, and I accepted him and I know he forgave me. But there was still something, and I didn't know what it was. I started learning by reading my own books, and listening to the messages and going to the different services. I learned a lot of things about prayer and after a few years I got offered an opportunity to go to another city in the South. I went to minister and also manage a bookstore. So I stayed there for one year, but we had some issues come up with one of the directors there. Because I was under him, I also got the bad end of the stick. It discouraged me, so I packed my stuff and I left.

I ended up back in my hometown with my mom and dad. One of the brothers gave me permission to sleep in his room and he would sleep on the couch. I started going to the church services for about two years after I came back. Then after a while I started missing some of my brothers. My brothers were out there. They weren't homeless, but they would go out in the streets and use drugs and all that. My curiosity started and I got curious enough to where I wanted to use some.

I was thirty when I had my first fix. They told me I was gonna get addicted and I did. After that first fix, I managed to stay away from it, but then came another urge that I wanted to taste, like at the beginning. I started going out by myself at night and my brother would cry because he didn't want me to be an addict, so I had to go it on my own From there, I ended up back in a shelter.

I stayed there for a few years. I left with my heart full of ambition and for all the right things. But I just couldn't get the support I needed. I couldn't find the support to go help me establish a goal for my life. I grew up by myself without really knowing anything. Everything I know is basically self-learned. My dad wasn't around when I was out there doing all these things I became a heroin addict. I was working at times and was able to support my habit. Then after a period of time, I lost interest in working and decided to get things the easy way. So, I started stealing and doing all kinds of crazy things to support my drug habit.

It was an off and on experience for me because I knew what my desires were, and it wasn't to be a junkie, and it wasn't to be an addict. I wanted to be a minister and do ministry work. But every time that I committed myself to these programs I felt like I wasn't getting anywhere. I would be discouraged and would end up back in the streets using heroin, selling everything that I had.

I lost everything. Dignity and self-respect. I lost it all. And now I'm here looking for help.

When I started sleeping on the sidewalks, I had cardboard and some dirty blankets for covers. I found myself in a trance. I used a lot of drugs to block out what I was doing. I would do drugs to escape from seeing myself as homeless. I got Hepatitis C from dirty "cookers" while sleeping in vacant buildings. Most of those items are contaminated with Hepatitis, but at the time I didn't really care. I didn't pay attention to those types of consequences. Now, I just want to take care of my health.

People who are homeless are miserable and they want a way out. I wanted a way out. I thought about committing suicide, I wanted to commit suicide, but I never had the nerve to do it.

I tried finding a girlfriend, but I didn't think anyone would appreciate having a boyfriend that was homeless, so that discouraged me.

You know, it's hard to be out there in the streets when it's raining, and it's cold, and you don't have a place where you can warm yourself up or have food you can eat - any kind of meal to get something in your stomach. When I was out there in the streets, some days I would go without food, and just be hungry. I was not able to get what I wanted because nobody wanted to hire me. I wasn't clean and I wasn't shaved or anything like that. I didn't have the proper attire, tools, transportation, all that's needed for a job. So that kept me out in the streets for a long period.

Nobody told me to go out there and live in the streets. I think that my condition was self-imposed. Mainly because of the shameless things I did. The guilt of what I had done. It took hold of me and I found that I needed these people out here. They didn't know who I was or where I came from.

I got to make friends and acquaintances. I would hang around with them. Some would end up dead and some would end up in the hospital, just sick because of their tendency to use a lot of alcohol.

On the streets, people gave me the looks that said, "You don't belong in a place." They ask you to leave. Like you're panhandling or doing something like trying to rob someone or steal something.

I do have some adventures from living in the streets. Stealing, riding on my bike, having people chase me after I'd come out of the store with stolen stuff. It got to the point where I was panhandling out on the streets. That's something that for me was kind of embarrassing. People that would drive by and see that I wasn't eating and would give me a dollar. For me it is degrading, to have to do that. I don't want that. I'm trying to better my life now and I still have those memories.

I have to think of what I want, what my situation is, and weigh the difference of what's good and what's bad. The good outweighs the bad. But, it's like a bug that keeps following me. I can't get it, I can't get it. And then when you get rid of it, the next thing you know, it's there again. And then you get rid of it again and it's there again. It's just like a bug that keeps following me. And it's like a cycle.

That's what I'm afraid of. Relapsing back into that lifestyle. To relapse and go through the same issues again, and all that. I don't want to have to go through relapse. I want to be able to get it right this time. I'm hoping that I will. I've made an effort inside me and God knows how much it means to me to stay clean and sober, so I can take care of myself.

I really am lonely. I don't know anybody who I can go to their house and live with them. I don't trust myself. And I don't trust other people. The streets make you real defensive. People wanted to help me, but I resisted. I rejected the help. I didn't accept it. I thought they were after something. I thought they would try to use me.

I remember one time when I was living at a shelter. It would be cold and I didn't have a job. There are people that hire daily workers. Day work. They really don't care about who they pick up or if you are a good worker. They just buy you some food and you get the job done. They'll put you in the back of the truck, even if it's 20 degrees or 30 degrees. Sometimes they don't pay you and that was discouraging. People try to use you because you're homeless. Try to take you for whatever they want. That's something that keeps a person down. I learned to look for people that will pay you.

It's like a trap. I'm in it. I'm in a maze and I can't find my way out. I became depressed. I never knew that I was in need of so many things in my life. Being neglected, rejected, unloved, uncared for. But I haven't given up on myself yet.

My dad wasn't a quitter and if anything, I'm going to learn from him. My dad was disabled from diabetes, he was evicted, and they had to amputate both of his legs, but he didn't give up. He kept going. He would still get up, move around get in his wheelchair; go to restaurants and other stuff like that. I'm pretty much just trying to tell myself, "Don't give up."

I tell myself that I care about myself, but I really don't care about myself. It's just the slow process of committing suicide. It's another way out. Out in the streets you don't know what's going to happen. But I'm learning to change my way of thinking. To change my heart's desire. Only God can help me there. There's a lot to learn and a lot to grasp. It can't be done in 3 or 6 months. It takes a lifetime. It's gonna take the rest of my life. So, I just have to do it one day at a time.

I wish people would consider us, not categorize us as minorities. Not discriminate against any individual. Look at the situation they are in. People should pay close attention to what their heart is saying. I'm not saying someone should be letting us live with them and take us in, but help come up with a way to meet these needs. Maybe we should put the product to the side and see what we can do for each other.

I want to get my life straightened out. Get my priorities right and reach out to fulfill my goals. My goal is to be a minister who understands a person and where they're coming from. The love of God is real. God forgave me and he has the power to do all kinds of stuff. I don't want to give up on his forgiveness and his mercy. It's kept me going and it'll keep me going. I want to do service to him and let people know.

Joey

———⟵∿⟶———

"I look back and wonder sometimes how the hell I managed to stay alive, but when you're on your high, anything is possible I guess."

One night I was selling, and I heard a gunshot. I was scared, so I ran through the street and under the bridge. It was dark, so dark, that I stepped on someone. It was the guy that got shot. I didn't know what to do, so I called 911 from a pay phone. Then I hung up and ran all the way to the south side of the city and hugged my son's mother. I told her what I was going through. She took me back. I was a wreck, crying. I explained to her that I didn't know what I would have done if I had stayed because I would have gotten caught with the drugs. However, since I left, I didn't know if he was okay. I told her, "I haven't slept. I'm hallucinating, seeing visions, shadows and hearing voices." She took me to the bathroom and had me lay in the tub. She washed me and tried to help alleviate the pain. I loved what she did for me that night and will never forget her for it.

So, I'm homeless. No, wait, I suffer from chronic homelessness. There's a difference between the two. For me it wasn't a choice, it was something I struggled with for a long time. I grew up in what many people would call a "not so normal" home. My mother was manic depressive and suffered from bipolar disorder. My two sisters also suffered from bipolar, so it was only a matter of time before the disease caught up with me.

My father wasn't around, and my stepdad beat the living shit out of my mom. He was an alcoholic and was diagnosed with cancer, so he had his own issues to worry about. It hurt to watch him beat my mom. He never touched my sisters, thank God, because they weren't around much. My oldest sister got pregnant at sixteen and my other sister was never home. She avoided home like the plague. Going to movies with her friends and hitting up the local hot spots at that time were better than being home.

My mother took care of me during the first phase of my mental breakdown. There were many phases, and they still haunt me to this day. I stopped taking showers, I wouldn't eat, and sleeping was difficult because I was already suffering from insomnia. Growing up, I was selling drugs, crack mostly, and I believe a lot of my problems steamed from this addiction. I guess I'll never know if it was the drugs or my own genetic makeup. For much of my illness, I had a lot of hallucinations. I would think that the pigeons were talking to me and I would hear random voices coming from things that couldn't talk. I didn't follow through with my medication, simply because I didn't think I needed it or I got lazy.

I sold drugs for about seven years before I was emancipated, and I was living in and out of my mother's home and the local shelter. I tried living with my real dad once, but he was never around, as a truck driver he was always traveling. He also had a drug problem. He was addicted to heroin and was selling it. It was at this point in my life that I tried to get a job. I landed an externship coming out of a job placement program, but my illness kept me from making sane decisions. For instance, I would show up looking like crazy at work. I'd wear a nice shirt and tie and show up with my pajama bottoms and slippers. No one took me seriously. I went to a local hotel after that and drank all week. I knew times were bad when my debit card was declined for insufficient funds.

This was when homelessness became somewhat freedom for me. I say that because I didn't have any bills to pay, no car to put gas in. Being homeless was cheaper than dealing with life situations and daily living issues. I didn't have to worry at the end of the day; I could just walk everywhere. The challenges I faced were constantly being around drugs and the urge to use, sell, and not get caught by the police. I don't enjoy being homeless; it makes me feel lazy, and honestly, I am bored a lot of the time. It's a pain. I learned the hard way that I should have continued school, not gotten into drugs, and stayed on top of my medical records. I finally was approved for SSI at twenty-two.

My goal in life is to go back to school and get my son back in my life again. Oh yes, I have a son, and my dream is to see him again. I do not want him going through the same issues I went through or what my dad has gone through. At this point in my life, I know I need help.

My biggest fear is stability and staying sober. I do not know how long it will last. Sometimes I think my paranoia will get the best of me; and I will be in a crowd and get frantic, or think something or someone is behind me, or the birds are talking to me kind of thing. I ask God, "What's going on with me? Why is this happening?" Then I tell myself to shut up. Get over it. I don't like to take medication to help me through my illness I become immune to it sometimes because I've taken it for so long. To get through my paranoia I just laugh and tell myself to "get the fuck over it." I've been sober for four years now. I look back and wonder sometimes how the hell I managed to stay alive, but when you're on your high, anything is possible I guess. When I was addicted, people said I was a product of my own environment. Well, in my environment, I was a product, and it wasn't something like a soda that you buy in a store, it was something that hurts and kills people.

Ever since
ThaT DAY
Amber BATHED
ME I look
AT HER AlWAYS
AS BIgger
THAN I
THE MOTHER
oF My child

By Joey

Heather

"I want to be successful. I have dreams."

I grew up in the South. I grew up in a very abusive background: neglected, abandoned, black sheep, rejected. I found Jesus when I was seven. I found His love and His grace. I was book smart. A's and B's in school. I enjoyed going to school; it helped me forget about what was happening at home. I didn't have many friends. I was teased because of my crazy hair, big bifocals, being big. That was miserable for me.

I finally met my dad when I was 15. I also met my stepmom and four sisters, but they rejected me too. They felt as though I intruded into their space. It was really rough growing up.

I met my husband when I was 18 and got pregnant. I was married for six months before I got divorced. Then I became a Certified Nursing Assistant (CNA). I was a single mother raising my daughter, sharing custody with her father. When I was 21, I got pregnant with my son. I stopped drinking and my mom wanted me to move back home. My son was born on Halloween.

When he was six months old I was severely raped. After that I got pregnant with my youngest and I moved north to where my father resides. I lost my grandma in the summer of 2008 and that's when my schizophrenia kicked in.

I had a nervous breakdown and my family was trying to take my kids from me. They succeeded and then I moved back south. I started smoking weed and started drinking again. Life without my children seemed very hopeless.

God told me to move to another city in the South. He said, "You will be homeless and the guy you're going there for will leave you, but go. I have big things in store for you." I've been through the ringer here, in this homelessness, but it's taught me a lot too. Two years ago, I started into heavier drugs to deal with the pain and hurt. But I have been sober now for one month.

Homelessness has taught me how to be more humble, how to love, and how to reach the unreachable. I have learned that everything I have is temporary and nothing compares to what I will have in Heaven.

Homelessness helped me find myself. I'm finding myself right now. It's helping me learn about my schizophrenia, my mental illness. I'm not proud of turning to drugs, but the experience teaches me what my mom was maybe going through and what my family went through. I see it in a different perspective now: How hard it is when you are addicted.

I was diagnosed with schizophrenia when I was 25. When I was younger I would have dreams which would come true the next day. My mom did fortune telling and reading cards, but I didn't believe in it. I would pray to God that he would take away the dreams because they scared me.

It started happening again when my grandma passed away. I was really spiritual and I didn't see it as schizophrenia. I just saw God telling me that I was going to go through some things with my children. That He was giving me warnings and I didn't know how to react to it.

I've seen my family plotting to separate me and my children. My sister said I was crazy and that I tried to smother Kelly, my baby, with a pillow. I really believed that my sisters were jealous of the relationship I had with my children. I think they didn't want to see me happy.

I don't have all the answers or the understanding of it all until the day I see Jesus, but I do believe that if God never did this and I never became homeless I wouldn't have any gratitude for anything. Maybe I would be one of those that would laugh at the homeless, make fun of the homeless, be ignorant and not understand them, not have compassion. Homelessness is teaching me to have compassion; it's teaching me to love. It has brought me closer to Jesus.

At one time I had started giving up and losing my faith because it seemed like the roads would never stop and nothing would ever give in for me, but I had to totally hit rock bottom so God can make me who he wants me to be. I believe that you can't understand somebody or something unless you've really truly been through it.

I want to be a counselor or a psychiatrist; I want to help the hurt. I want to help the ones that have been forgotten and I believe this is the journey I had to take so I can have the experience to understand.

I've almost been murdered three times and my family doesn't even know. I fell into some abusive relationships, but I'm really trying to break those generational curses and cycles. It really starts with me and if I don't do it then there's a chance that my children are going to go through it. I can prevent them from having a bad childhood. What if my mental illness got so bad that I got frustrated and just took it out on them? What if I wasn't the mother they know I am?

The last thing I told my son was that Momma is sick. It was his fourth birthday. He goes, "Momma sick" and I said, "Yeah, Momma is sick and you can't come home yet." He said, "Okay." That was really rough.

I didn't understand it before, but with my experience now, five years into my illness, I have a better grip of it. A better understanding. I can catch the triggers now and I know what sets me off. I can see the patterns. If I was busy being a mom and doing all the stressful things that comes with motherhood, maybe I wouldn't be as healthy as I am. Maybe I would be sicker than I am.

I've been on my medicine for two months. I'm not in that mind frame of, "Oh I don't need this medicine." Even though I feel so great, I need it daily. When I was homeless I was not taking my medication for several reasons. Denying my illness, feeling ashamed of my illness, feeling confused, and believing I don't have an illness when truly I did.

I believe my schizophrenia has played a part in my becoming homeless. My family just shut the door on me. When I was a child they tried to say that I was bipolar from all of the trauma I suffered. It makes sense - one minute I'm happy and next minute I'm sad.

I never was one to lash out in anger, but a few times recently I became very angered, very bitter. I had given up on the Lord and I was tired of drugs and I was tired of the life the drugs gave me. I decided to come to a program at a shelter.

I went to a retreat last week about forgiveness; forgiving yourself and forgiving others. I really felt I finally let go of the past five years: the grief of my grandma, the loss of my children. It still hurts and is painful, but I have to get healthy for me first and then my children. I don't want the day to come when my children are looking for me and I'm sitting under a bridge or they knock on the door and I'm hitting the crack pipe.

I want to be successful. I have dreams. I dream about working with children, in the ministry. Reach the people who are forgotten.

I feel like a lot of people are homeless because of what they have been through from childhood all the way up. A lot of hurt people, a lot of pained people, and a lot of neglected and abandoned. If I wasn't a part of it I would not have understood it.

I want a home again with people coming over and barbecuing, fellowship, and celebrating birthday parties. I am slowly, but surely getting there. I have to work on myself first and a big part of that is working on my mental health. If I'm not healthy mentally then I will not be healthy when it's time to reunite with my children. What was done to me was very unjust from childhood all the way up into adulthood, but God has a powerful testimony.

I remember just getting tired of looking for that next hit. That was the turning point for me. What can I do now when I have no money? What can I do to get that next hit? I didn't want to prostitute, not wanting to lower myself. I was just tired. Street tired. I was tired of living in the streets feeling dirty knowing that I was better than this. Just thinking, "This is not where I belong. No, I don't want this life and no, I don't want it to get any darker than what it is. I got to change it."

I spent a lot of time with God. A lot of time praying and not giving up. Then slowly things started moving in my life and the next thing I know, I've been blessed left and right and He has been showing me His love. The streets don't love me. I love the streets - they don't love me. I love the drug, they don't love me. They wanted to destroy me. I was getting tired of the drugs not doing what they did at first and I was close to opening the door to heroin. That's when I said it was enough. I'm trying to break the cycle before it is 10-20 years of drug use like my mother. My mother is still on drugs and she's 50. I don't want that for me or my children.

You have to adapt to a new way of living when you are homeless. You are so used to a certain way of living and you are set in your ways and when you are homeless you can't eat what you want or as much as you want. You have to shower with a bunch of people. You have to think about all the germs, diseases, attitudes, characters, rapists, sex offenders, and murderers. It's one of those lives in which you live in paranoia and wonder if someone is going to come get you from behind. Constantly. Somebody stealing from you, like your wallet, and then trying to recover your IDs and social. Then when you are able to recover it, it's taken from you again. Just the hassle of trying to get back on your feet. Sometimes it just feels like you're running in a complete circle.

At first it was really affecting my schizophrenia with being overwhelmed and stressed out all the time. It was triggering my schizophrenia. It was challenging for me, going in and out of the hospitals and watching friends that you get close to passing away due to drugs or getting hit by a car or murdered or everyday life events that you don't think you will be subject to. Getting beat up, watching women get beat up, watching severe violence everywhere and living in fear; it is very hard to adapt to.

At first I was successful having a place, and then I'm all of a sudden homeless and I can't keep a home, because I can't find something that fits my income. One of my biggest challenges is staying off drugs when I'm disappointed, when I'm hurting, and when I'm feeling certain ways. To not run to that drug.

Hopelessness is not a fun feeling, but now I'm full of hope for my future and I'm slowly getting back to the girl I used to know and everybody knows. It's been a challenge to find her and show unconditional love to anybody when I'm hurting so bad. We serve a merciful God and full of grace and forgiveness and understanding and a just God. I just want to shine so bright. I sometimes feel like a little girl in a corner with no light shining and then sometimes I feel that girl shines her light so bright!

I want people to remember there's hope even when you don't feel like there is. You are never alone; God is always with you carrying you through your storms. Don't give up on yourself; keep pushing through. Believe in yourself and know that struggles are only temporary.

I want to find me. To practice my recovery in mental illness. To stay sober. To get my GED. And to start working again. I want to have a place that I can call my own and see my children. I want to change lives and work in a shelter as an advocate and help other people succeed in getting out of homelessness. I want to go to college for psychiatry and reconcile with my family. I want to send for my mom and sister to come and visit and just have the means to do those kinds of things.

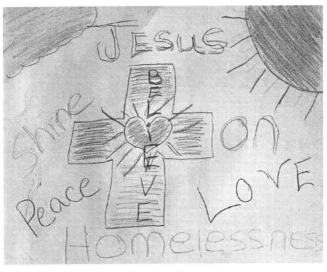

By Heather

Darren

"I played for two presidential inaugural parades…"

It is probably difficult for you to believe, but I am a college graduate. I went to a university in the South. My family was the first generation to move into a city. My family before was raised on farms. We did very well living as upper middle class. We were fairly successful. I had what I wanted. I was not needy as a child. I mean, I did not have anything extravagant, but it was enough. If I asked for more, I knew that it was not right. We were not raised that way. My parents were very good people. When they became very ill, I knew I had to drop everything to help them out. That was a difficult time.

As a child, I was into music. I began taking drum lessons when I was eleven and have been playing ever since. I am fifty-six now. For the past forty-five years, music has been my passion. I did everything band related in school. When I went to college it was only right to major in Music Education. I taught middle and high school bands for over twenty two years. However, it was not easy getting there. My twin sister and brother did okay for themselves, but I was very angry. The other kids seemed to be learning things a lot quicker in the classroom. I always had to study extra hard. What kept me from advancing was my learning disability. It is called Attention Deficit Hyper Activity Disorder (ADHD). This made it difficult for me to concentrate in school. I was placed in special classes, and I also had a speech therapist. My mind would go very fast, faster than I could speak, and as a result, my words would come out non-comprehendible. When the school decided to test me, I ended up being placed in 4th grade when I was supposed to be in 6th grade with my sister. I would now be two years behind her. She was much smarter though, she deserved it.

You see, back then, no one knew what was wrong with me. I did not even know what was wrong with me. I remember just being told that I was always acting out. As a result, I always got the belt and was whipped. I didn't even realize I had done something wrong. Now I know I cannot blame them for spanking me. They had no idea that my actions were sometimes out of my control. My ADHD coupled with my depression made it difficult to keep up with everyone academically. Although difficult, I was able to make it and graduate from college. College life was great. I was given many opportunities, being part of the band, to travel. I played for two presidential inaugural parades with our university marching band. I still made the Dean's list every semester.

I didn't meet many people. I feel like sometimes I just didn't fit in or relate to them. I was single and didn't have any children. But I was making great money. The state paid me over fifty thousand with my level of experience as a band teacher. So when my parents both suffered a heart attack simultaneously, it was easier for me to move back home to care for them. It was only right. I resigned, terminated my teaching contract, and moved back home. This was in my mid-forties. My mother was left in a wheel chair and my father was never the same. It was planned for me to care for them for about three or four years, then place them in a nice living facility. However, that never happened. Nine years had passed when I had to bury my father, then my mother a week later. I grew into a deeper depression. I went into a lot of debt. My brother and sister each had a family and found it difficult to help. I felt like I lost it all. I could not even file for bankruptcy because that too cost money. I was left in a lot of debt.

I moved home in 2002 to care for my parents. When I lost everything, I realized that I could not afford to care for myself either. The apartment I moved to was $785 a month. It had to be on the ground floor because I couldn't climb up stairs and stuff because of my disability. I looked, but it was so hard to find an apartment. I found out I couldn't live on $1,250 a month of disability. I could not ask for help either. I didn't realize that something had festered between me and my sister. I would see her maybe once or twice a year on holidays and spring break. She was very mean to me and it hurt me a lot. I had to give up everything, everything I had. My brother was a little bit standoffish too. I apparently said or did something that upset them over the years. I had over eighteen thousand dollars' worth of instruments. My sister was supposed to store them for me. She said, however, she was going to move to a smaller house and sell them for extra income. I didn't think it was fair that she was going to sell the instruments that I worked for and paid for over twenty-two years, so I took my $2,800 French horn and $1,200 trumpet. I needed to sell them in order to make money for myself. I only received $250. That's all they paid me.

That's how I ended up in a homeless shelter. Not able to relate to a lot of people. I am on anti-depressant, anti-anxiety, and anti-seizure medications. I have mild seizures. I will go to a blank then I will come back and I don't know what was going on and you wouldn't even recognize it. Most people in here do not have the education that I have. I do not have a criminal record. I have never been an alcoholic or drug addict. I just don't fit in.

By Darren

Freedom

By Emily

Freedom is one that I want and I crave
Yet all the cocaine just gets in the way…
My life and my mind begin to distort
It's hard to believe I can't even snort…
The needle the rush has all been too much
I've lived in a world with friends who all sux…
They are selfish and vail, evil yet wise
They'll take all your cash and feed you such lies…
When I'm down and all out they always stop by
With a hand full of dope and that look in their eye…
"But only for cash" … they express with such greed!
What will I do if I can't get it free…
That fix in our life so many embrace
Will not drag me down I refuse to decay
My life's been so little and yet, been so much
I begin to love life and not so much drugs…
Thank you Jesus.
Amen

Sahara

"You're constantly thinking of ways to get out of here, but I can't leave because I know I don't have anywhere else to go."

I'm originally from a southern town. All my family is over there, including my two daughters and my son. I moved to a larger city because there were no jobs there. I was a provider at the time and they were just not hiring anyone at that time – it was going on 3 years, and I was living with my mom and my sister.

My mom brought me in and told me she didn't want me on the streets, but my sister was being a pain in the butt. She took me in for a while, but then around Thanksgiving she kicked me out. I was on the streets for about three months, which was a horrible experience. After that a friend allowed me to stay with him. All I had to do was talk to his mother and his mother allowed it, but after 3 months I decided to look for a job being a house keeper.

I've done housekeeping at hotels, but never going into people's houses. It was hard for me to want to do it, but I went ahead and did it anyway. And after a few months went by I had to leave those people's homes. There were a lot of little things going on that were inappropriate and I just didn't belong there. I left and went back to my mom's house. My sister got upset again that I was there, and I said: "Whatever happened to the family thing, the *'mi casa es su casa'*?" She just wasn't willing to go along with that. I know she had moved on in her own life, so I understood. No more harsh words between us were exchanged.

I got another job working with a couple on a ranch. I enjoyed staying with them and working with them because they were really nice people. It was so peaceful in the country. It was so beautiful, but the scary thing was the snakes and the scorpions and the fact that there were people out there hunting for deer! I had to be careful going outside when they were hunting because you never know when they'll think you're a deer and accidentally shoot you! The job only lasted for a short period of time. I started in July and it ended in December. The same week I stopped working with those people I moved back to the city, and it was the best decision ever!

I used to live in the city over 30 years ago. I had my two sons here. I got a job as a caregiver and was working there for almost 2 years. I couldn't believe how fast the time went. I was taking care of some old ladies, but their daughters were just terrible to deal with. They were saying, "Oh, you're not taking care of my mother! Oh, you're not doing this and that." They were just really hard to get along with. After almost two years they let me go.

It had been hard taking care of the people and watching them die. I never thought it would affect me, but it did. I got close to them and then when you're watching them, oh, my God, I would close their eyes because I knew they were passing away. Watching them die was so hard. I didn't know that it was going to affect me in such a way and, before I knew it, I started not wanting to be there anymore.

The daughter thought I wasn't good enough to take care of her mom anymore. She didn't fire me - she gave me a severance pay and let me go. When she let me go, I had nowhere else to go. I had been living with these women and taking care of them seven days a week.

It was kind of scary to go to a shelter, but I had nowhere else to go and I didn't want to be sleeping in the streets. Right now I'm waiting on other programs that help people find apartments, but they have run out of funds. I can't get a job because I applied for disability for the mental issues that I have. You're constantly thinking of ways to get out of here, but I can't leave because I know I don't have anywhere else to go.

It just baffles me. Whatever happened to our family, our loved ones? It's all changed. It's not the same when family would bring you in if you were going to be homeless. My sister decided she was moving on, and worrying about me wasn't part of her plan. I love my family and everything, but I told my mother: "I'm not going to go by for a while. I'll call you to let you know I'm okay."

My family knows I am in a shelter. My mother still asks me: "Are you still there?" I say: "Yes mom, I'm still here, still waiting." I have to be patient with these people so I'm not on the streets anymore. It's been a challenge, but it's going to be great. All of my friends tell me I can make it on my own, and I hope so and I pray on it and just continue to be patient. That's all I can do really, but it's hard having to sit around and wait. And so it's kind of tough, but I'm okay with it and I've been dealing with it for all this time. I believe in God and pray to God to be patient, so I'm being as patient as I can.

There are a lot of people that are negative. It's kind of hard to be around negative thinkers because it's hard to be positive when they're negative. But you can't listen to them because you have to believe in your heart that you're going to get out of here and you're going to make it. It's not going to happen overnight, but it sure will happen in the future. I believe it's God-sent and if it wasn't for my son and his girlfriend telling me where to go I don't know where I'd be.

A lot of homeless people have mental health issues and it gets kind of hard not to do something about it. I'm bipolar, I have anxiety and depression, and have been diagnosed with schizoaffective. That's kind of a combination of what's happening to me. At first it was hard to deal with being all alone, and my family didn't want me. I was so depressed at the time and was not on any medication. It had been a while since I had been on medications because I kept denying that anything was wrong with me. I'm on medication now and it's being controlled and it helps. Sometimes the condition I have causes me to be depressed, but that's the way it goes with the medications. The medications help me out a lot;

they keep me feeling sane, make me feel good. They help me believe that I can still go out there and make it on my own even though I have my mental issues.

God, the Lord has helped me get through. I would pray to him every night and say, "God, this place is horrible." It's something that's hard to deal with but this is the place we're at and I just have to be patient until I get out of here.

Homelessness is a serious matter and it can happen to anyone. You can be homeless in one day. People lose their job; how will you pay for things like rent and bills? There are so many young people living in the streets right now, it's sad.

People judge, like why are you homeless? I don't like that. For one, I lost my job and I had nowhere else to go. People who are homeless are trying to survive. The available places can't hold everyone that's homeless. That's why there are some people in the streets asking for money, doing what they have to do to survive. The police come and tell us here that we can't do that anymore, ask for money, they told us we'll get tickets. I think you can even get put in jail for soliciting! But there are people that have a heart and give to those in need. I think some people have gotten used to being homeless all their life, and they don't know any other way. A lot of us got kicked out of our homes and can't be with our family.

I pray for my children to never be in the position I'm in. I have two daughters and two sons, but one passed away recently. They all have their own things going on but we keep in touch.

I guess I can understand how it was hard for my sister to take me in financially. I was an extra person to take care of and she had to kick me out. Maybe she was trying to push me to start taking care of myself, but if it was me, I'd bring my family in from the streets. I have one brother and four sisters. We talk every now and then, but I miss hanging out with them. Everyone knows I'm here, and they ask how I ended up there but I just never wanted to be a burden on them because they're married and have their own stuff going on.

It's all up to the person. It's up to you if you want to make a better life. Just because things don't happen as fast as you want, you have to believe, you have to be patient and work it out so you won't be on the streets. I want to go to school and become a medical assistant or maybe study psychology – I'd love to learn more about it. It sounds like a really interesting subject. I used to deny mental health issues. I never wanted to take medicine, but now I'm more positive about the way I am and I know I need to take my medicine. Sometimes I think about just jumping right into school. I want to learn and get wisdom- keep the focus knowing that I can make it and be successful.

Jeffrey

—⟶ᴍᴏᴄᴇᴛᴏᴄᴛᴇᴏᴏᴍ ⟵—

"I was walking down the street. I told God: 'I'm tired. I need help. I want to stop.'"

I'm from a big city in the South. I'm 43 years old. I've got five brothers and six sisters and I'm the youngest. I'm the youngest out of eleven. So pretty much, I've been spoiled and handed things throughout my life.... Pretty much kind of played into my adulthood. And that's when all of the problems - ... some of the problems occurred.

I went into the military. I come from a military family. I went to school and played sports and became good at it; basketball and football. I had a scholarship to a state university, but I didn't go through with it. I played against a future NBA player. That was back in 1988, '89, '90 in high school. Yeah, I was pretty good at basketball, but my scholarship was in football. I was a point guard and in football I played tailback and receiver. They said a school was looking at me, but I didn't go through with it. I wasn't interested.

I had a good childhood. I was close with my family. My parents are deceased. I was close to my brothers and sisters. We love each other from a distance, due to my substance abuse. I can't blame them. What I did it was on me. My oldest brother got killed in Vietnam before I was born. And my other brother passed away with heart complications. The second older brother just passed away not too long ago. And my third brother also died.

Some of my most memorable childhood experiences were cookouts, barbecues with my family, and Christmas. Man, that was nice. And my birthday - Halloween right next to it. I celebrated pretty good all the way around. Thanksgiving cooking, smelling chitterlings on the stove. Nothing like mom's cooking. It was awesome. I enjoyed the time with my parents. I believe if they were still alive I would be a different person today. I got swept by the streets, man. I put myself out there. I've held good jobs, but my substance abuse interfered a lot.

The shelter I am at has been good for me. I've had help in the past, but I haven't taken advantage of it. I'm on medication and it helps to keep me calm. I can be pretty hyper. I'm trying to use coping skills. Good coping skills - positive coping skills. I'm trying to stay away from people who use drugs. People won't give you food or money, but they'll give you drugs.

When I want to relax and chill I like to take walks. I like to read books, look at a good movie, and spend time with my female friends. Kick it with them. We can talk and laugh. I like to relax. I read the Bible, too. I was in a ministry. That's when I really learned the word of God. And it was a big, big help with my walk with Christ. I see members on the street from time to time passing out the Word. I used to teach in the church when we had a little sermon that we had put together. They use to call me Mr. Jeffrey. My brother - he passed, he was a pastor. I've really been thinking about how I can change my life. I read the Bible when I get the chance.

So you want to know how I became homeless. Well, when my parents passed I had to get out of the house. My sister went over to the house and I was on drugs and alcohol. And I've stolen from the house and pawned stuff. So my sister said she did not want me at the house until I changed my way of living. I chose the streets. I left and then I stayed in the streets and that's how I became homeless. I had some friends that I moved in with. I went from my friend's house to my brother's house.

I've dealt drugs, done drugs, hung out late at night with the wrong crowd. I've been standing on the street in the middle of a drive by. I'm not saying my friends are bad, you know, I'm there too. What does that make me? So we feed off each other. I thought I could get help. I am trying to get my life straightened out so I moved to a shelter. But first I moved in with my brother - he helped me.

So I moved in with my brother. I thank God for him because he helped me out. He gave me a place; put a roof over my head. He didn't want me out on the streets. But he passed away. So I moved on because my sister in-law was tripping about me being there. That showed me how close family… they shouldn't be like that.

I moved to sleeping outside a shelter. I've been doing this on and off. That is where all the homeless people go. I stayed there for about a year. A little bit over a year, on and off. Then I moved to a program in the shelter. Being around a lot of people like that is so congested, so I'm here now. But there are more positive people around the program and more structure.

When I was using drugs, my drugs of choice were crack and weed. I started that many years ago. I started that when I was about 26. I'm 42 now. I don't know how I persevered this long. I know it was God that preserved me. I got health problems. I have major high blood pressure. Other than my psychological diagnosis, blood pressure is my big problem. That's the killer right there. I'm on medication, so I got to stay on that medicine. My diagnosis is PTSD, MDD - major depressive disorder; psychotic. Not psychotic, that's going crazy. I take psychotic medication… stuff like that.

I've had some nice female friends that I've messed up because of my addiction. I've traveled a lot. I've been all over the West. Well, I met this young lady and we hit it off. She took me away from here and I didn't do drugs or get involved with drugs while I was with her.

She was a good woman. It was just me. It was alcohol. I didn't want to do drugs. It seems like I have control over it except when I'm around people doing drugs. See I wasn't around anybody that was doing it. She didn't do that stuff. She was an RN. Yes, she was big time! She was a sweet lady you know. She was a traveling nurse. At the time I was dealing drugs.

She showed me another world. She tried but I messed that up. Other relationships that I had in the past I've messed up because I want to do what I wanted to do instead of being like 50-50. I was always thinking about myself. I'm not a selfish person, but when I'm on drugs and alcohol I want stuff and I want it right then and there. And I don't care. I'm a very good hearted person. I was raised like that. I come from a good family. I've lost friends, too. Cool people that wanted to help me out. Yeah, but they cut me off. I mean like my brothers and sisters.

We talk from a distance. We love each other from a distance. As a matter of fact I'll be having lunch with my brother next week. He's real cool. All of them are cool but we are kind of tight. He's in his fifties, he's an older brother. He kind of knows - he's been with me when I was going through my drug addiction. He would see me out in the street and would stop and say, "Hey man, come here and talk to me."

He would give me money and food. He didn't have to, but I'm his brother. He felt bad seeing me like that. I thank God for my brother. Like I said I'm a cool person. When you're in that cycle it's like a washing machine. Just going in circles. When am I going to get out and go into the dryer and draw myself off, cool down, and live right? In the dryer, you clean. That's when you clean. And in the washer you get washed. Yeah, that just came in my head. And you know all that dirt is washed out of you. That's why you got to get washed before you go into the dryer.

I've always worked. I've been working since I was 18. My first job was at a fast food place. Did good. Stayed there for about three years. Moved up into a leadership position. Did real good. I was young, full of energy. I've always had good jobs. Mostly cooking jobs - and I was a manager there, too. And I went into the military. I got popped with marijuana in my urine. Back then in the military there was zero-tolerance. It was my fault, it was a party that I had for myself. I thought I would be cleaned by taking these pills that would clean me out, but they didn't work and I popped positive. I was about 27 years old. My mom passed in 1999 and I've been in and out of homelessness since then.

Homeless people have good survivalist skills and they are not always judgmental. People don't like me because I'm homeless. It's something that just happened to me. It doesn't dictate how you were raised up before you were homeless. I'm just homeless *now*.

I've been hungry before. Lunch trucks would come up and you can go over and get a sack lunch. You know what it was - that addiction - that got me to that point. To that gray area . . . you know, that's all that I can pinpoint. That, and then my family arguing saying that I shouldn't be doing the things I was doing. You know, going to jail, getting in trouble. I've been to prison and the state jail. I had some crack in my hand and the cops stopped me. I was smoking a joint. That was my second time. I spent six months in jail and six months in prison. There were other times for marijuana. I got off on that because I completed my three-month probation.

I felt like an animal in a cage while in jail and in prison. It wasn't fun being locked up and having the guards tell you when to eat and when to go to bed. There are a lot of people and you don't have privacy. It's what it's made for: animals.

I tried to stay clean for a while. I try to maintain. But then I'd fall back. I went to jail mostly for possession, not selling.

My number one need is God. I'm in a program at this shelter. The program is steering me the right way. I get substance abuse counseling and my medication is being taken on time and that is very important. The medication helps me. I'm more focused, I'm more alert. I'm not just thinking about drugs all the time. I'm thinking about my future and this program is pushing me towards that.

I'm going to apply for SSDI and I am going to apply for work part-time. I want to do some things that will keep me occupied. I'm ready to live on my own, I'm tired. I've been dealing with this for a long time. I have lived on my own before, we own duplexes and rent houses. My family owns them and I didn't have to pay rent while my mother was living. She would just say give me something when I got paid and I would just give her money. I wasn't really a renter but I stayed there.

My brother is over the rental property now. So everything worked out. I've always had something, I didn't just fall out of the sky. I pretty much got everything I wanted. I grew up with my nephews and nieces and we were tight. I come from a good family. I worked for what I wanted and I bought my first car. I bought it and I put in it my dad's name but I paid for the insurance and payments.

That's when I was working at a veteran's community. Man there was some good people there. Veterans, war veterans. I had a good job there. I stayed there for about three years. I was treated very good. I was a waiter. To hear stories from them and to hear the stories they would tell me. Wow, and some of the things that happen to them. They would help me with anything, but I had a job. They just like me so much because I was always respectful: "Yes, sir. No, sir. Yes, ma'am."

I used to live in the deep South for about two years. I went through a lot of old ordeals over there because I made a lot of money. I was working and fixing houses. I do carpentry. I got some skills. I can do ceramic tile, sheet rock. I'm pretty good at what I do, but when I was there it was the drugs. Partying every day. I didn't stay clean over there. I mean, I wanted to. I met some good people, real good people. I lived good, ate good, but I didn't save any money. Money was just flying out of my hands. There was a lot of work. I had so much work. We really never ran out of work. We always had something to do.

When did I realize I wanted to do something about being homeless? When I was walking down the street and talking to myself. I didn't look good and I didn't dress nice. I was down and out, drinking a beer by myself. Then I said, "Man, I'm tired." I told God: "I'm tired. I need help. I want to stop." So I went to a shelter and cleaned up and got some clothes. Looking the way I was looking - and that was last year.

My hopes and dreams for the future is to live like Jeffrey should live. Jeffrey is going to live good. He is going to live like a king. Substance abuse is out the window because I can't be me and I can't live the way I should live and be the way I should be. This is me, today.

Eclipsed

By Christy

To me this means
Through the light
And the dark…
How they mesh
In order to survive and
Feeling trapped.
I've been through a lot
Of dark times through
My life and somehow I
Got through.

Chris

———⌇⌇⌇———

"Being homeless, it just happened."

I grew up in a nicer part of town in a large city in the South. I used to live with my dad. My mom left when I was little. My dad raised and cared for all 6 of us. I guess my most memorable childhood experience was being happy when my dad was alive. I did not worry a lot and just enjoyed life. I enjoyed playing pool, hanging out at the arcades, listening to music, exercising, and reading.

Being homeless, it just happened. I didn't expect it, it just happened.

I was staying with a couple of friends. We used to stay in motel rooms and we would pay up for like a whole week. Everything was good at first. Then one of my friends started having problems with his girlfriend. He stopped going to work and I was pretty much paying for everything. That put a lot of stress on me so I went to a crisis center and I stayed there for a week. I was sent to a hospital for two weeks and after that I stayed with my brother. He said I could live with him; however, after a while I needed my own space. He has kids and they need their own space, too. They said it was not an inconvenience to them, but my nieces are growing up. I understood that; you can't live with someone for the rest of your life.

A caseworker came and moved me to a respite care facility and I stayed there for four months. I was transferred from there into a program at a shelter. This program has been good. They work with the courts, paid some of my tickets, and helped me get an ID and Social Security card. They helped me get back on my feet. Although they were able to help me with a lot, I was able to get a job on my own.

I didn't like it at first; you're around a lot of strange people. You can only get along with a certain amount of people. Everyone is different which makes it difficult to get along with him or her. Everyone is going through something that you don't know about. You don't know what to expect and it's hard to trust people. From my experience it's hard to trust people. Some people say that they are good for this and that, but when it comes down to it, they only worry about themselves. Nobody looks out for each other. There are a few people that are reliable. If I need to borrow money or someone borrows money from me and he or she pays me back; I don't have to go looking for them. Then there are some that don't pay you back.

I was diagnosed with some type of mental health disorder. I told the doctor that he can write whatever he wants. They observe you and they write whatever they want anyway; they make up stuff. He said, "No, we always keep an eye on everybody to make sure everybody's doing fine." He was writing stuff that did not even describe me.

I was upset.

They said I had all these mental problems and they prescribed me all these medications. I was taking medications. Instead of the medications working they started doing the opposite. I wasn't able to see clear. My vision was blurry. I was shaking all the time - just pretty much lost. "Take your meds," the doctors said. "Take your meds." But I just felt worse.

There's nothing wrong with being homeless. Some people make bad choices but it's best to make good choices because everything you do has consequences. No matter where you go you're always going to have someone that is in charge whether you like it or not.

As far as moving forward, I'm used to taking care of myself. A lot. Due to my legal history it is difficult finding an apartment. I'm ready to step up and make good decisions. I took a graphing class, so I would like to be an architect or work drawing for comic books.

Mavrick

"I want people to know that homelessness is not fun."

From the time I was born to 1985, I lived in a large city in the South. Then from 1985 to 1995 I lived in a different city in the Southeast. After that I lived in several small and large cities throughout the South and the North.

I had a breakdown, went to the hospital and they did all these tests on me and found out I had pulmonary hypertension, heart and lungs. I spent six months there, got out and had another mental breakdown so they put me in the psychiatric ward for like 2-3 months. From the psychiatric ward they brought me to a program in the shelter.

Of all the places I've ever been, I liked the North. The weather was nice. It has a beautiful countryside and mountains. I like being out in open spaces. I can stand cities but I'd rather be out in open spaces.

I have three stepsisters. Last time I heard, one stepsister, the baby, just had another baby. She's 21 and she's had three kids. She married a guy who already had three kids. Now all together it's six kids. My middle sister, as far as I know, is still in the state federal penitentiary. I don't know why. I don't have a relationship with her. Then my other sister, I've only met her once, so I have no idea what she's doing.

My childhood was kind of blah. I could remember a lot of memories but not really any good ones. Most of the time it was just... "you did this, you did that, you're worthless."

"Yeah well screw you too!" Smack! "Hit me again!" Hit me again then I have a bruised knee cap. Yeah so I had a rough childhood, no big deal.

I enjoy movies and books. My favorite genre is horror movies and favorite book is fantasy sci-fi. I'll basically watch anything. Right now, me and couple of other guys are going to a comic book store. On Wednesdays and every other Saturday we play Dungeons and Dragons. We have been doing that for about a month or two now. It lets us get out and get away from here. Other times, to relax, I sleep or I just let my mind wander.

My experience of homelessness began when my mother died. I had a mental breakdown. My depression played a role in me becoming homeless.

I hit my boss. I ran out of money to pay my rent, so I turned in the keys and moved back home. I was going to stay with my grandma, but she had just broken her hip so I was like "aww crap." It's not the first time that I have been homeless so I know how to survive on the streets and I did until I got put in the hospital.

While being homeless, I lost a lot of weight and just learned how to survive out in the streets. Just do what you have to do to survive. But I grew up in the country so I know how to live off the land.

My lack of income makes it difficult for me to stop being homeless. I'm waiting for my income.

My hopes are to get out of this shelter and not come back. I've been here almost a year. I'm waiting for my SSI to come in. Once I get my income I'm outta here.

I look forward to leaving. I've been doing this program since December 2013, I'm more than excited about leaving this place. I just want to get out of here.

I do socialize with the people here. Not a whole group. There are probably 5-10 people I socialize with.

If I had to go somewhere else for an emergency, it would probably be with my grandma or my step-dad.

I haven't really reached out to my grandma because of her new husband; me and him don't really see eye to eye. My past temper has made it kind of strenuous on their relationship and I don't want to push it any further. So I'm thinking more of her than me. I'm trying to be considerate.

There are a lot of misunderstandings and stereotypes that people have toward people who are homeless. They think homeless people are dirty and bums. It's not that, we are just like everybody else. It's just that we have a harder time fitting in with the community because of all the stereotypes. I can be dressed nice to the nines, walk down the street, everybody thinks I'm not homeless. You know I have actually done that. I have nice clothes on and start talking to regular people and I tell them I am homeless and they tell me "you're not homeless" and I'm like "yeah… yeah I'm homeless;" it's stereotyping.

Stereotypes interfere with everything. I've actually tried getting jobs, but they don't want to even bother with me. I'm a good worker, but what can I do.

A huge challenge for me in my homeless experiences and in general has been sleep. Sleep is a big deal.

With me, I need sound in the background to help me sleep. Like a radio or television set. I had an iPhone and I had the iHeart radio app on it so I would listen to it until someone jacked my phone one day and now it is really hard to fall asleep. I got people making noise by snoring (and) grunting, but that just aggravates me. So now I just think of things until I fall asleep and that's usually around 3 o'clock in the morning.

Before getting here, when I was on the streets I would go to the hospitals, and sit in the visitation rooms. I would be in there, up all night, drinking coffee, drinking tea, watching TV. Or I would go to the library. I would go down there grab a book, go outside and just sleep. I knew where to sleep. I knew where to get food. There were places I would go to eat. I ate good, but I lost a whole lot of weight.

There were bars I could go to sometimes. They would serve food. There were restaurants. I knew people that worked there. I could just be sitting there and they would give me a sample. I was at fast food place around 1:30 in the morning, and one of my buddies came up there and handed me a big platter of nacho supreme. So I didn't go hungry. If I did I just drank a whole lot of liquid to fill me up, coffee, hot chocolate, and tea. I survived.

The problem was the cigarette situation. I'm a smoker. I admit it, I did steal. All I stole was cigarettes. That's it. Which is kind of easy if you think about it. I've done that like 20 times. I've probably ripped that store off at least $500 worth of cigarettes, easy. Don't get me wrong, I'm not proud of it, but you got to do what you got to do to survive. Like I said I'm not proud of it. It's over and done with.

Labor is basically a temp job. They send you out to do different odd jobs. It lasts for a day to two days max. The only reason why I am not doing that anymore is because my heart and lung condition. Plus, the money they paid you was below minimum wage.

Last time I got any money from my family was for my birthday. My grandma sent me 25 bucks. Other than that I haven't asked for money. They say everything I need is here. I got a bed, clothes; I got prewashing, if I need a bus card, I have that, too.

I want people to know that homelessness is not fun. If you have family, be nice to them or else they will turn their back on you and tell you to get the hell out.

Also, I want people to know that they need to make sure they take their meds. That's most important. Take your meds. In case you are homeless and want to get out, take your meds. They'll keep you stable. Sometimes they'll keep you stable. Like me, I take my meds and I'm still unstable.

Polly

"That doesn't make me weak, it makes me unique."

"3 hots and a cot." I'm sure you've never heard that expression before. Three meals per day and a bed, this signifies security. Something I never had. I was 14 years old when I became homeless. My hometown was country as hell. I was the second oldest of twelve. Eleven brothers and myself, you could only imagine the segregation I felt. I was raised in a household where my brothers did not have to live by the rules. Myself, however, I had a curfew which was at 6:30 pm and I completed numerous chores and practically raised my younger brothers. At the time, I lived with my grandparents. I would consistently ask my grandparents why I was the only one who did chores, and they told me it was because I was a girl. It was unfair, it was wrong. I was molested at 14, by one of my brothers. At that point, I became angry and was tired of the abuse. Being the only girl in a home of all boys gets to you. I don't know where my brothers reside today; I only keep in contact with one of them. I decided to run away. I lived on the streets for 3 years in a cardboard box I found outside of a restaurant. I was lonely a lot of the time, but I did continue to visit friends throughout the town. I called myself a "black sheep" because I strayed and everyone stayed. But I'm okay being the black sheep. Although it was uncomfortable, no one wanted me. That's what made me sad.

To survive, I would pick pocket from local stores and steal anything. Anything I could use, strings, food and clothes. I was caught shoplifting and spent 6 months in jail, but again "3 hots and a cot." I had a place to sleep, I was warm and there was food. The hardest part was not seeing my friends.

I was 17 when I got pregnant. I fell in love young, with a dance instructor named Walter. He never stayed in my life; once he found out I was pregnant, he packed up and left. That was the last time I saw him. After he left, I hit a state of depression and went looking for my mom. I found her, surprisingly, and she introduced me to drugs. Weed, cocaine, alcohol, synthetic morphine, we did it all together. She was more of a best friend than a mom. She took me out to the bars, and I hung around a very old crowd. At 19, I found her on the floor over dosing from the drugs. This was the scariest thing to witness. She pointed to her watch and whispered she was dying. I felt empty inside.

She passed away and I gave birth not too long after, to a girl I named Katy. At this point in my life, I felt like I had a purpose. I knew how to take care of this child because I spent my childhood raising my brothers; however, I left her to live with my aunt and uncle because I couldn't stand being in my hometown anymore. The memories were too much to handle.

I decided to move to live with my father and his wife at the time. I got on the Greyhound and met him. I was introduced to my step mom, who was a short Hispanic woman who spoke broken English. She didn't like me from day one. After 2 months of living with them, she kicked me out because I had abandoned my child.

Looking for stability was hard. I got a job as a waitress, and I was fortunate enough to stay with my friends. I was back on drugs at this point, because my manager would invite me to smoke pot with him, do some speed and drink occasionally with him. He would tell me that doing drugs would make me a better waitress and "clean better." I left that job after some time and ended up bartending, which I made decent money doing. Enough for me to get an apartment and help get me back on my feet. However, I still struggled with my drug problem and suffered from bipolar disorder.

I was officially diagnosed after my second pregnancy. I couldn't keep a job, pay my bills, or take care of myself. I take medication for it now, and reading books helps, but this disease is something I will have to deal with for the rest of my life.

I had 4 children during the time of my bipolar state. Alan, Sam, Junior, and Matt. Sam, Junior, and Matt all passed away because of a degenerative disease. The gene runs in my family, but I didn't expect to lose three children to the disease. I found out a few years later that Sam's dad committed suicide. He jumped off the bridge. I don't keep in contact with my other children's fathers. I feel it is for the best. The children are now grown up and live their lives separate from me. It's been awhile since I have seen them. I occasionally feel suicidal and depressed. Here at the shelter they have taught me good coping skills such as walking away when a bad situation arises and then returning to it with a clearer mind.

Homelessness is horrible. You never know what or where you're going next. Your next shower, meal, anything. The longest I went without food or a shower was two weeks. I didn't want to go to a shelter because they are very inconvenient with certain times they are open, occupancy allowable, and who is and isn't permitted.

My biggest struggles are overcoming the deaths of my children, handling my bipolar disorder and the constant feelings of loneliness. My goal at this point is to have self-worth. I now know my boundaries, I have found stability and I am in a meaningful relationship. But I will never forget my life as a "black sheep." That doesn't make me weak; it makes me unique.

Tony

*"What I want people in America to know about
homelessness is that for one thing, it is a struggle"*

I was born in a big city in the South. I was living with
my dad and real mom. I was living with them for a while
and went to elementary school. My parents separated. After
that my real mom went to live with her mom in the country.

I lived with my dad because my mom's mom has a
mental condition. My mom couldn't take care of me. I
started taking drugs in high school, thinking it would make
things better. Then my dad gave me a job when I got out of
high school. I helped, I was doing alright for a while, but
then I started drinking and going back to the drugs.

At first I was smoking weed then it went to cocaine.
I got tired of that. I got used to it and it wasn't doing
anything. I then went to crystal meth. After that I just quit
because I got tired of all of it. I wanted a better life. I always

knew that I just wanted a better life. I was probably 33 when I stopped and I am 35 right now.

I lived with my aunt for a while. I was trying to get a disability check. They asked me to go see a doctor. The doctor told me that I didn't qualify for it because I wasn't bad enough. It's because I knew how to live and take care of myself. After living with my aunt for a while, I moved back to my dad's and things were going alright for a while. My step-mom and I didn't get along very well. At this point I was about 25 or 26 years old.

I have a brother who is now 26. My parents I really took really good care of us. They always made sure I had clothes, food, and that I was safe. They always made sure I went to school. They were just good parents. If I were to recall a bad memory that stands out, it would have to be when my parents got a divorce.

I believe the divorce affected me big time. I started throwing fits and getting in trouble at school. I was in Special Ed classes because I was not motivated. I believe I didn't know how to handle that so I just acted out. I was just angry and frustrated.

Meditating I guess helped me. I watch some TV, but I'm not a big TV person. I watch about 34 minutes of it, but then I have to get up. Unless it's a movie I will watch a whole movie. Another thing I like to do is play basketball, walk downtown and talk to people, but I get tired of things easily.

I was first diagnosed with bipolar (disorder) when I was about 16. I did not handle the diagnosis very well. At first I would take the medicine and then I started with cocaine to try and forget about things. Prescribed medicine was just not working and that is why I went with what I knew would work with me. After a while I got tired of cocaine and I went back with the prescribed medicine.

I never knew they had shelters. Back then I was not aware of support groups. I wish doctors would have told me about all the options that were out there. The support could have helped me with taking my medicine and giving me advice.

When I was living at my dad's house, I started doing crystal meth again. My dad knew what I was doing. He was asking me what my problem was and what was going on with me. I don't know why but I have always been afraid to talk to my dad. I just don't think he understands me. My step-mom decided to give me a haircut one day. When she did she took a hair follicle and had it sent to a lab to be tested - that is how they found out about my drugs.

Shortly after that the guy I was buying the drugs from showed up to my house and told my dad that I owed him money for the drugs. My dad has custody of my niece and nephews, so he didn't want me at the house anymore. That is how I became homeless.

My dad did try to find me help. He wanted me to seek help. He got on the computer and tried to find the help for me. I was 34 when he kicked me out.

I guess being bipolar has a lot do with the reasons that resulted in me being homeless. I can't express myself. I jump around quite a bit and make bad decisions. I start thinking about the things I need to do and I lose my appetite. I feel like it has affected me in keeping jobs or even getting jobs. I can't keep my job for a while because one day I just get tired of it and I don't want to be there anymore. I don't necessarily get fired, I just lose interest and it is my fault for deciding to leave.

What I want people in America to know about homelessness is that, for one thing it is a struggle. Most people that are homeless might not realize all the options they have. I didn't know the options I have now were out there. They should just know that people that are homeless just need help and options. It is a struggle. I would tell them to check out a shelter. We just feel lost that we cannot explain ourselves at times. There are some people that are happy with being homeless. They are comfortable. Everyone is different.

The main thing that makes it difficult to stop being homeless is my bipolar. I feel like I need to be here because of the counselors and groups. All this is helping and I don't ever recall having that.

Some of my hopes and dreams for the future include getting a job, keeping it, and getting an apartment. I want to make my dad proud and show him that I can do it. I wouldn't say live my life for him, but I would like to get his acceptance, just to have it. I would probably get a good reaction from him because of that. I just also want to be able to manage my bipolar. I want to do the best that I can do.

On a perfect day, first I would get up, get a cup of coffee, and smoke a cigarette. Then I would go back inside and play with my niece and nephew. Take care of them. I would lay them down for nap. I would sweep and mop the house. I would do chores in the house. After that I would wait for my dad to get home and we would eat supper as a family. That's about it really. It is not too much to ask for.

Untitled

By Mari

Once there was a little girl,
Whom could not understand others.
Everyone around her, did things she
Could not comprehend.

Any wrong behavior that went unnoticed,
She took into adulthood.
This was before the man she loved,
Took away her childhood.
How could she revile him, when
He had lifted her life.

He taught her to enjoy the snow,
Which made the world sparkle like diamonds.
So, later she did the same with her boys,
Taught them the joys of tossing snow.

Never did she understand,
that her mind was flawed,
until she was stricken by a stroke.
Then, she began to finally see, what God
Had tried to show her, that the flawed
Mind, was mine.

Since I was a child of abuse and neglect,
I learned to overcompensate in the areas
I had in my control.

I was a great student, and did my very best.
My teacher's always loved me, so
I was called the teacher's pet.
Never did I feel offended, when
Other's called me a pet.

Just do not touch me, for a knuckle
sandwich you would get. Touching was
not permitted, without my consent.

Control was taken from me, by all
Whom I loved, when they would tell
My story, which opens the door, to
More disrespect.

There is more to tell you about my life,
Since I do not know you, this is all
You get.

Alex

—⁓∙⚬∙◦∙◦∙◦∙⚬∙⁓—

*"It's hard. This constant battle I'm in, fighting to
understand what is real and what's a delusion. This
constant battle between reality and this darkness that
is always with me."*

It's hard for me to get myself across to other people.
There are a lot of words which I use that to me mean
different things than they do to other people. It's hard. This
constant battle I'm in, fighting to understand what is real
and what's a delusion. This constant battle between reality
and this darkness that is always with me.

I had to get away from my family. I felt stuck with them.
They're violent, brutal, and verbally abusive. Thank God,
nothing ever happened to me. The first time I heard them
argue, it hit me just like that: I didn't have the ability to take
pain like other people do. I was so fragile. If I had a broken
arm, the sky fell. There would be no way for me to come

back, no reality for me. Everybody else would have their reality of, "I went through this and I got out, everything's okay now." But me, I would be stuck in my own reality.

I was diagnosed with schizophrenia when I was eighteen. I noticed something was wrong with me the first time I knew I could breathe, when I knew I could see, and I knew I was alive. Once I was old enough to understand all things, like, "Oh man, I'm alive. What do I wanna do?" I knew there was a problem right away because my mind wasn't thinking correctly, it was running too fast. My dad put me on hyper pills and I got over that, but man, it was violent - verbally - because I can't take pain.

Most people have the ability to take pain and they can go through struggles and say, "I went through this." But for me when I look at it: "That's what you want to go through. Those are the choices you made for yourself to go through. You may not consciously know about it, but subconsciously those are the choices you make." I don't feel sad for people who don't make it because it's their own fault.

At first I was sad because I didn't know any better. I was sad for everybody, even for criminals who were locked up, behind bars, for doing the things they did. Back then, I didn't know any better. I thought everyone was kind, everyone was nice. It's as if this spell was cast over us. Now I know better so I'm only going to feel bad for myself. All the people who I love, they can take care of themselves. They don't need me in their lives. I know for a fact that if something goes wrong with my life, it's over.

I know how much I can go through, and it's not even that much. If I get a broken leg tomorrow, everyone else is going to be happy. Me, I'm going to be around everyone else feeling sad with a broken leg, but the sky would fall on me. And I wouldn't be in the world with everyone, I would be in *another* world *with* everyone. It's not fair.

I consider myself nice. The first words that came out of my mouth, I can honestly say were nice. The second thing I thought about was what could happen to me if I was nice. A lot of bad things. It's like I have this fantasy of something bad, something evil, lurking. It probably doesn't exist, but what if it did eventually one day. Maybe never, but who knows? That's child talk, but I always worry about that as if it's going to come.

What if this darkness, this evil, was to possess me? At first I'd live okay for a while, have everything, probably go through the struggles of life. I could even tell my story, but when I least expect it, I would be in hell. Where evil rules me.

I don't consider myself a half-crooked person or a half-nice person, I can say I'm just nice and I feel like the only way I can make it is with love.

If only I could do it on my own, but I'm always going to have this issue where my mind wanders off into another reality and I think it's real. This reality, this darkness, where evil triumphs over nice things. Nice is never going to win. I'm nice, I'm never going to win. I've got a long time ahead of me of love or pain.

Another person, a doctor might say, they're just delusions, but they're *my* delusions. Who are you to say they're not real? It's been hard because I've always carried this thought with me: I'm a nice person, evil's out there, it probably doesn't exist, and I'm crazy. People look at me like I'm crazy. I think to myself, "I'm going to beat this crazy person that you think I am, and watch me make it to where I realize it's all in my head, a fantasy, just delusions."

I'm never going to forget how it felt to have evil lurk over my shoulder. It feels so real. As a little child I would walk with bricks on my shoulders, thinking that it would never be okay. I'm always going to have that fear which spooks me. Unless a miracle happens, and I finally become free of this darkness, this other reality. I'm always going to carry that. People don't know how it feels, but maybe they will one day.

I'm good at heart, but it's hard because I take people's stuff in all the time, all the bullshit. I just want to get a break. I want to knock them upside the head and be like, "Hey man, who are you really because right now I can't see anything. I can see you, I see him, I see everything, but I can't tell if it's trying to hurt me. I can't tell if it's real or if it's just in my head. Until a miracle happens and someone comes along and says, "Hey man, here's the right vision for you," pats me on the back, and says, "Here's how the world works, it's not the way you think it is." I would say, "Alright, I'll take that." See, I don't want reality to be the way *I* think it is.

I learned to accept that they could be delusions. I learned to accept that they are delusions. I use these skills to gain knowledge, to find where I need to go, and to gain people that I need to meet. Even if I'm not going through it, I learn it anyway because there's a chance that I could go through it one day.

I was in a city in the South and I told myself, "I've got to get out of here." My whole family was starting to split from the house and I wasn't going to be able to pay the bills by myself. I told myself, "These have to be just delusions you're going through, about evil and being nice, and evil coming into your world and taking you away from all your loved ones; and yet you're still there with them. They don't know you're gone." I told myself, "These have to be just delusions and I've got to get back to the homeless shelter because I know that's the only place right now that would help me."

I told myself, "It's time to buckle up, you're going to have to." I got down myself, but it was in a positive way. It wasn't like "if you don't do this, that's it, final count." I just woke up and said, "You know what, mom drop me off at the homeless shelter because that's the only choice I've got right now."

I could have stayed with them. I could have gone with my aunt, but I didn't want to do that. I wanted to go on my own, make it on my own, and get my own things. That way I could come back to my family and tell them, "Hey, it's been a while since I've seen you. I got on my feet, I'm doing good now, let's go to the house and have a BBQ."

I want my family to smile when they see me again. So I became part of this mental health program at the homeless shelter, hoping that I could make it happen. Every day since I've got here, I've been constantly keeping myself in check, trying. There have been some rough times when I miss my family, but I don't let it bother me. I just let it glimpse over me. I go through it. And I tell myself, "That's enough dude, you gotta dust it off your shoulders, you gotta wake up."

When I was young I didn't really have anybody telling me what to do in life. I just pretty much had to pick up after the scraps that were taught to me. I just had to pick up as much information as I could from all the violence and all the verbal abuse that was going on. I tried to pick up any positive I could from all the negativity that was going on around me. I feel like I turned out alright. There may be some people that I don't like. I can't make you like me and I can't make myself like you.

My life has been interesting. Very interesting because I learned a lot from strangers, not from my own family. It's complicated because you wouldn't necessarily use this knowledge. These strangers, they were teaching me a different type of knowledge. A type that made me feel like I was enjoying my life. I wouldn't call it the type of knowledge that you get from school. It was more like street knowledge. To me it was important.

One day, I got into an argument with my mom. She didn't want me around so she kicked me out. Maybe it's because I have a disability she didn't know how to handle. I was mad because *I* can't even handle it sometimes. She just threw me out and said, "Hey, you gotta go, I can't handle you, you need to go." I said "alright I'll leave." I left on the streets and forget it. I'm not trying to live like that. It was hard. I thought, "Is this is how you're going to treat someone when they really need help?" No.

I just feel sad when the day comes that *they* need help, anybody needs help. I'm going to have a house to come into and everyone is going to be scratching to get in, but I'm only going to let a few people in. The rest, I'm going to let the jungle have them, but I would try to get everybody in.

It's crazy because no matter how bad a situation gets, there's always people saying, "Well it's alright, it's alright." No. It's not alright. It's not. Maybe it will be alright, but it's not alright. I wish someone that's not in my shoes, that didn't go through any situations like I did, that was always okay, could understand what I went through. I'd rather have that person come up to me and tell me, "I can understand what you went through." If it's another person who went through a struggle, I don't want to hear it from them.

It's not fair because I don't have the ability to take pain. These people who go through struggles and situations, they still find a way to make it pop, to make action go on. Me? I have nothing going for myself except for a grave. I'm just gonna get old.

I'm not trying to live like that. I'm trying to work these last thirty years that I have left it in me. And retire so that at least I can die peacefully.

Being homeless, it was just hard. I had people, strangers, introduce themselves to me, ones that were homeless or ones that were once homeless. If they hadn't come to me, I would probably have just passed out on the street because I was out there for a few days. They brought me into their house. They gave me a place to stay. It was pretty cool, but it didn't last that long. I went to the homeless shelter then I went somewhere else.

If it wasn't for the other people on the street seeing what I was going through, trusting me just by looking at me walk by, I'd probably still be on the streets right now. I see myself this great thing, this great fighter who defeats this thing. This darkness which tries to hurt me, but in reality I thought, "God, it's a lot harder than it seems," because at that time I was homeless.

What if that darkness had put me in years of homelessness? I wouldn't be able to make it. It was heavy, it was hot, scary, and if it wasn't for the other people on the streets who would look at me and say, "Hey, need some water. Need a place to go?" They were always there. I always had that help.

I had strangers help me out and I got to meet them. I got to go to one of their houses, in this little room. I stayed there for like four weeks, then the homeless shelter, then my mom came for me and we went back home. The relationship between me and my mom is just crazy. She's not someone I can really depend on if my life was on the line.

I don't know how else to describe my homeless experience, because pretty much everyone's stories sound the same. I really have no words for it, but it was bad. It was very bad. I don't want to live like that for no reason. And I *was* living like that for no reason.

I remember being homeless for like three days when I was sixteen. I stayed at an abandoned house, had my clothes, blanket. My mom had kicked me out. Then I went back. She said, "I didn't kick you out." I was like, "yeah you did, you kicked me out. That's why I left, if you hadn't kicked me out I wouldn't have left."

I don't think my mental health was the reason I was homeless. It was the people around me. I have my schizophrenic moments, but they're only triggered by the people around me. It gets bad. I just get so angry. I live a messed up life as it is already because I don't have that life where I can just snap my fingers and have everything there. That's the life I'm used to. I don't care if that wasn't the life I was born into.

It's just fishy to me, this world, people that act like it's the perfect world, where everything's okay. You better have something behind that card you're playing, and it better be something good because right now the card you're playing isn't good, you telling me that everything's all good.

I could handle my disability fine as long as I have support, friends to help me get through it. It would be perfect, but I'm in a world with nothing but strangers and then there is my family, which I think are strangers to me anyway. Everyone's a stranger and I can't work with my disability. I'm always angry because I don't know who you are.

Then the world looks like chaos. People are getting sold in sex trades and stuff like that. Then you have this other part that's all good and shiny where everyone's living well. Then there are people dying from AIDS and stuff.

My mind is very fragile. I could believe in something that other people believe in, but it wouldn't be the same. I would ask myself, "Could this be real?" And they would be like, "It's real, it is real." They have a different type of brain cell or something. I don't care if it's real or not. As long as over all I'm doing good. That's all that matters now because I tried to put everything in the right path. It's not working, so I'm just going to take care of me.

Boyfriend-girlfriend relationships aren't going to work out for me anymore. I'm going to stay single and I'm going to have money. The way I see females, they're part of the reason why I am the way I am today too and why I'm making the choices I am to make myself better.

At first, I could start a family when I was young. I thought I'd start a family, have sons, daughters, and keep on going, stop or whatever. As I grew older, I saw women cheating on their boyfriends. The ones that do make to where you stay together forever, I never see them and even when I do see them, there's always some type of friction.

I'm looking for that relationship where there is no friction, no cheating, and there is no putting your babies on child support and all that.

I did want kids, but I don't want my kids growing up in a life like this. They're not going to be born in a world like this. I don't want my sons to see how women act and I don't want my daughters seeing how men act. I have a plan for myself: Die old, die peaceful.

I can literally say that I have learned from everything in this world. Even if it's eating a plate of food. I can learn from it and get better at what I'm doing. It could be anything because all my knowledge, everything I am, there's a reason for it before it comes to me and I see it. I'm aware of the possibilities that may happen.

The one thing I would want people to know if they were to ever be homeless is that everything is going to be alright. You're going to make it in the end. You're going to have that smile, that happiness. You're going to have that dream you always wanted, that you always thought about, that you could never accomplish. That's what I would want them to know.

In order to make it on my own, I would need myself to be fully intact. I'm still learning. I would need myself to fully understand how the world works. That's one thing I need to know. I also need to know how to make the right choices. The first thing I would need to do is understand myself and understand how the world works. I can go off of that. That would be one step. The second thing I would need is support from people who want to make things happen. I would need people. A third thing I would need is to figure out a way to keep it going for other people. To teach them how to get started in doing the same thing we did.

Hopes and dreams for my future? I just hope to start a family. My dream is to be in a loving place where I can support my family and help my kids grow, where I don't have to worry about violence and things like that. Just to have a family, and just to grow properly, the way a family should grow up. I just never had that. I never had the feeling of having a son or a daughter or even a wife because of the way the girls grew up where I'm from, and what every relationship I've seen has been through. That's what I would hope and dream of.

That way if my kids ever needed anything I could say, "Hey man, I got it." Then they could look at me and say, "Man, my dad is the best," and my wife could say smiling, "Look at my husband, he's so good to our kids."

By Jacob

Diane

—⁓∿∘⊙⟋⊙⟍⊙∘⁓—

*"I feel like I am in this puddle that I just can't get
out of and every time I go to get out, my feelings mess
it up."*

Living at this shelter has taught me a lot about myself.
I have been here for about three months now. I have been
homeless for about three years, moving from friend's house
to friend's house. I have been a waitress my entire life. I had
to give it up because my feet were falling apart. My pain,
along with my mental disabilities, started to get worse. I
couldn't keep a job more than two or three years at a time.
I would always end up having some kind of blow up.

I am diagnosed with Bipolar II and Obsessive
Compulsive Disorder. It was difficult growing up. I was
raised in a military family. My adoptive father is a retired
Lieutenant Colonel. He shot my mother when I was ten. She
died twice, but came through. Although I did not witness

it, I could tell it was bad. I awoke to bright lights and loud sirens. My father was not even arrested. I guess he was able to convince the police that my mother shot herself. The reports later showed that there was no way that she shot herself. I did not know how to deal with it. I guess it was covered up as a result because he was a high ranking officer. I just believed what I was told.

I reacted by smoking pot when I was twelve, and I began to slit my wrist when I was thirteen. It was when I turned eighteen that I started to get into the strong stuff and shooting up. I remember doing this to get my dad's attention. I wanted to hurt him somehow. I remember he made threats to my mother that he would hurt her. I didn't want anything to happen to her. So I tried to do what I could to get his attention off of her. I became very close to my mom because of it.

Life has always been difficult. All the men in my life have really hurt me: my father, my husband. I shot up drugs from age 18 to 26, and I had to stop when I went to prison. At age 40 I was released, but I started right back up again. You know when they say addiction is life long? It doesn't stop. I went over ten years without it. When I got out of prison, everyone treated me like a criminal. I got rejected by everyone. I felt disowned. Even my kids lived with my husband. He did drugs too. I was in so much emotional pain I did not want to go on. It was like, if I didn't take what I needed, I would not be able to function.

But I am human, I have strong values. I am proud of my daughter. I don't know how she turned out so perfect. She is involved with many school activities, and she is just beautiful, strong, and smart. My son lives with his dad and step mom; but they are obviously involved with the drug system as well. It upsets me because he is not being raised to my values; but I know it is difficult. I am not stable right now.

I am in this shelter now. This is the first time in my entire life that I am getting help – I mean actually getting the help I really need. My goal is to be as stable as possible so that I can get a place where I can take care of my mom. I think my mental condition plays a big part in my stability and emotional pain. People don't realize the emotional pain and what it does to a person. The rejection from my father, my mother, my husband, my son has all made me feel so bad. I feel like I am in this puddle that I just can't get out of and every time I go to get out, my feelings mess it up. I am on the right medication, and this is the first time that I feel the stability that I need. Many doctors before would keep prescribing me the same thing even though it did not work for me.

I just want stability, just to be stable and pay my rent and recover from my eventual foot surgery. Most people fall and stay homelessness because their mental health is out of their control – not because of their income. Some people just have more resources, others don't have any.

Izzie

"I would scream but there was nobody."

I was born in Latin America. I had four sisters, and my dad was a doctor. My family left in the 1960s. The properties were taken away so we pretty much left with nothing. It was just my dad, mom, and four little girls. From there we traveled, moved around a bit. My dad was able to find a job in a mining hospital without his medical licensure because you can't use it here. We finally settled down in the States where my dad could get his medical licensure and get his practice going again. I was eight when we settled down in a large city in the South. My dad was the first Spanish speaking pediatrician there, so he did very well for himself. I had a really nice life.

My sisters are a lot older than I am, so I did not really grow up with them. They went off to college when I was still a little thing. So I grew up alone, a spoiled little brat, pretty much with my mom and dad. My dad worked a lot. My mother was German, very domineering, a good woman, but with a very strong temperament. I had a really nice life. I was a little too spoiled.

When I was about sixteen my older sister got engaged. Her fiancée molested me when I was about fifteen or sixteen for some years. I never told anybody; like most kids, I didn't want to say anything. He used to praise me and tell me how wonderful I was. I didn't know if I was ashamed or if it was good or bad, and I adored him. That went on for some years.

When I was eighteen he and my sister got married and left. They went far away, so that experience was buried. I went off to college. I already had trauma, I already had post-traumatic stress disorder. I didn't know. When I went off to college I didn't do well. I started having emotional problems and depression. My parents didn't know what was going on.

When I was eighteen, my parents decided they were going to take me on vacation to get away. When they took me out of the country, I was on a date and we didn't realize these drunks came up behind us. They tied us up, and then I got beat up and raped with a knife. I was about eighteen then. That vacation wasn't good. My parents didn't want to deal with it so they sent me to a doctor because I was pregnant. Then my life went on. I went on to college. I never finished. I was just a mess- depression and anxiety.

This went on for years. One bad relationship after another. By that time my sisters were all gone from the house. My sisters and I didn't get along. They didn't like me because they saw that I was a spoiled and preferred child. They resented me because I got everything that I wanted. My life was supposedly wonderful, but it wasn't that wonderful.

Years went on. It was on and off from school, no drugs, just emotional problems. Very bad emotional problems, unhappiness, and instability. My dad put me on many anti-depressants, but nothing seemed to help. It was just really bad.

I finally got married for the first time when I was 27. I ended up divorced ten years later. After my divorce, I came back to live with my parents, who had retired in another state where I finally finished college.

I did both my Bachelor's and my Master's there, but I couldn't get a job. I went to a national school for paralegal training. I thought I was going to love it, but it was like a secretarial thing. I have always been a social worker at heart because I have done that without a degree. It's always been in me. So I have always loved it. I have done it for years without the degree so I went back and got my Master's in social work. I was in my 30s by then.

I started working, got my home. My parents helped me buy my first house. I owned my home and I was doing really well, but the depression and the anxiety and stuff kept coming. By that time I knew what it was. I had been diagnosed with post-traumatic stress disorder. I knew what it was by then, but it wasn't getting any better.

I was put through all sorts of treatment modalities. There was one that was really good, but I didn't have any money. It was a something to do with stimulating your brain waves, neuro feedback. It was supposed to be something wonderful, but it was $300 a shot so I just couldn't afford it.

I would do well and I would do bad. When I looked for a relationship to make it better, for somebody to make me feel loved, it usually ended up badly. When my parents got sick I was in my late forties. That is when my life really went downhill because my mother was my life source. She was the one that would rescue me, the one that really understood.

When my mom got sick, that is when things got really bad. She got Hepatitis C. We don't know from where because she never used drugs or had a blood transfusion. At the beginning she was fine, but slowly she ended up with dementia. She lost her mind for a while.

At that time, I was working at hospice when my mother went. We had to put her in a psych ward and that is when everything just fell apart. I had a huge nervous breakdown and a car accident. I just couldn't manage anymore. I was living near my parents, not with them, and my sisters wouldn't talk to me. I had no communication with them. They wanted nothing to do with me. They thought I was a little brat that wasted money and whatever.

So I asked one of my mother's relatives to please call them about my mom. My sisters needed to come and help with my mom, to just be there. She called them and they refused to come because I was there. As long as I was around they did not want to see my mother. Another slap. So they didn't come.

My mother got really bad. I stopped working for a while. Then Mom got out. We got her on medication and she got better, but she couldn't take care of herself. My dad was elderly so we hired somebody to stay with them, until I ended up finally not working because I was just not well emotionally. I was not doing well. I stopped working to be with my mother all the time and, I think when my mother died I went through a big denial. To me she wasn't dead. There was nothing that mattered and I went on my merry way.

Then if finally hit me; my dad was very dependent. He was not as strong a person, so I was burdened. He couldn't care for himself emotionally or any way. So I started having problems with my dad. He didn't want to bathe, he got depressed. He wouldn't get out of bed, wouldn't talk to anybody. I didn't know what to do with my dad and my sisters wouldn't come.

My father was very quiet. He was not very emotional. I would tell him, "Dad, I love you," and he would say, "Thank you." He was not an expressive person at all. He was not somebody that you could hug and you would get a hug back.

I finally found a lady who would take care of him, be good with him, and could nurture him. I would come visit. He got sick and passed away.

When he passed away, I just couldn't handle life anymore. I didn't want to be alive because then I was really alone. My sisters didn't want me. Who did I have? Just me, oh and my house and my dogs, and my career; but I wasn't functional at that point.

My dad had left me an inheritance to live off of and I owned the house. I had my little car and everything. In the middle of all this depression, I decided that I was finally going to get married. Big mistake. I wanted somebody who would love me and take care of me. I found, according to me, a really charming and smart guy. So I ended up getting married.

He ended up a loss. He blew all the money that I had. Every last bit of the money I had went. I just sat there and watched it, did absolutely nothing. I was just there watching, oblivious in la-la land, waiting for someone to come and take care of me. I was pretending that everything was fine, but it really wasn't.

He moved us to South America with the money we had. He sold my house and everything. In South America, the beginning was wonderful. After two years we ran out of money. He started hitting me and beating me. And when we are out of money, we are out of money. I would sleep on the floor and had no food. That's how bad it was. I slept on a dirty mattress, on the floor, and there was no electricity

It got really, really bad. There was nobody there. Cow towns, who would you go to? There were no doctors. I had to stop taking my medication cold turkey. So I started having withdrawals, delusions, and hallucinations. I was aware that I was having them. I was aware that I was losing my mind and I kept screaming, "dear Lord, somebody help me." I would scream but there was nobody.

That went on for about two years. All I had was my three little dogs, a dirty mattress, and a fan. Seriously, that is all I had. No clothes even, I ran out of clothes. No medicine, nothing. There was no electricity most of the time so you had no TV. There was nothing. It was dirt poverty, just surviving on whatever we could find.

After about four years of that, I called one of my sisters to see if I could go live with her. She told me I wasn't her problem, and that I was an idiot for losing all the money, and that she didn't want anything to do with me. So I buried my family. I didn't want anything to do with my family after that.

After the fifth year I couldn't take it anymore- the tin roof in the houses, the heat. The heat goes up to over a 100, and you're inside that house. It is sweltering heat and it is horrible. I just couldn't take the heat, the humiliation, the hitting, and the "fat this and the fat that, you're an idiot for studying, and you're an asshole." I just couldn't stand it anymore. So I called one of my friends, a childhood friend from Home. She managed to get the American Embassy to pay for my plane ticket back. The American Embassy paid for my ticket back because I had nothing. I had two shorts and one shirt. I had nothing but a little Chihuahua- my little Izzy.

My friend helped. I came to live with her because my family wanted nothing to do with me and they still don't. They are angry at me because I lost the money.

My friend owns a home. She is divorced. I lived with her for about four months until I couldn't take all the things that happened to me. I just didn't know what to do with myself. I was just there. I didn't have a job, money, or anyone. I just had a dog. I had nothing and I thought, "Oh my God, I have nothing."

I went through another bad depression, had a really bad nervous breakdown. I started to bang the wall, pulling my hair, losing it completely, and I was isolated in her house. There was nobody around. After four months she said, "You are going to have to leave. I can't take this anymore. You're driving me crazy. I can't take it and I have to work." That is when I became homeless. My friend has my dog. She is taking care of her for me. I visit her every week now.

I've been at the shelter for a year. I would have been out if I had my paperwork. When I was in South America I lost my naturalization. I lost it, and you can't get a job without an ID. The process to get it back is expensive $400 or $500 for a replacement. I had no valid ID and I couldn't get anything renewed because I had been out of the country for so long.

The passport that got me back into the states expired. I didn't have money to renew it, so I came here with no ID, no nothing. I couldn't get anybody to help me pay for it either. I finally got my church to pay for it, but they only paid for it a month ago so it is going to take about four months more to get it.

When I get my paperwork I can leave and start working.

By Joey

Larry

*"I came from a good family and had a good life, but
my substance abuse took that all away."*

I've got a story that you might call fairly ugly. Parts of
it are very good, very nice. A good life. But parts of it are
not pretty to look at.

I was born in Europe, in Germany in 1946. My family
came to the United States after World War II, in August of
1947. We're a refugee family. My mother, father, brother,
grandmother, and my uncle and his family came through
Ellis Island in New York City when I was eleven months old.
We are all Holocaust survivors.

I had a good life. My father was an attorney and my
mother worked as a cultural liaison, helping writers, artists,
and performers who were new immigrants get established.
She helped them with whatever they needed. She helped

them adjust to life in America. I had a good life in the States.

Before I turned four my father passed away. My mother remarried about seven years later. My step dad was an executive director for a Jewish organization that helped people get to the United States and helped them out once they got here. My step father passed away. My uncle and my grandmother also passed away.

We moved to the South permanently in 1960 so the family could be together. I always had an interest in the arts, especially music and drama. I was in the music business as a performer until the middle of the 1970's. Things looked good. They looked bright. I had a lot of friends and acquaintances. I had succeeded in business and my friends were willing to help me. In fact, sometimes they requested my help.

In 1969 I got a call from some friends out West. I dropped out of college the week before final exams and went. I was already having substance abuse problems before I moved to the West coast.

I was part of the 60s generation and drug use was a part of my life. A part of a lot of people's lives. I ended up a heroin addict. I have been an addict for forty-six years. Substance abuse problems ruined everything and took everything from me.

I am not and have never been part of any gang or crime-related organization. But I have been in contact with people that were because it is part of the business aspect of the drug trade. It is very dangerous. I have been shot at and stabbed. I have been hospitalized for hepatitis C, but thankfully, it never got past that.

I came back to the South because I felt more comfortable there. I had friends in the business here. They are local, but well established. My substance abuse continued.

I lost my home, but not my family. My family was always there. I have been in and out of prison since 1978. The last time I was in prison I received an anonymous letter telling me that my mother was in a nursing home. She had an accident, then a stroke, and was in a nursing home. About a year later, while I was still in prison, I was notified that my mother had passed away. I was allowed to come back for the funeral.

While I was in prison I worked as a law library clerk. I'm educated, so that was kind of easy work for me and I enjoyed it. The prison administration and the warden were pretty familiar with me, as I had been in and out. We had a running joke about reserving a spot for me. After the funeral I was in prison for another two years. During that time I lost my home, which my uncle had built for us when we came to the South. He was a home builder and had a well-established business.

Like I said, I came from a good family and had a good life, but my substance abuse took that all away.

When I was finally released in 1997 I found a good office job -customer service work, selling over the telephone, technical support. Because of my addictive personality I was a workaholic as well. I did extra work after hours. I cleaned, would mow the lawn, and clean the fence line. I was making decent money back then. That lasted about four years, but I was still using heroin. It finally overtook everything.

I lost my apartment, began living with friends, and I was still on parole. During that time I stayed at a shelter, as a condition of my parole. My past made me familiar with the system, and, as they say, this wasn't my first rodeo and I knew how to play it. It never stopped me from living my life and continuing the lifestyle I was in.

After a while I was staying with a friend who had established his residence and I would pay rent. But things finally got out of hand, to the point where I was desperately seeking help. I voluntarily admitted myself to a psychiatric hospital over and over, but nothing had worked yet. It had been a life of making the wrong choices, but now it was becoming a matter of life and death.

In 2010 I was arrested again for possession of a controlled substance.

I kind of know how the legal judicial system works. I was able to talk to the district attorney and was granted five years of probation, rather than the maximum sentence of twenty years in the penitentiary. My probation ends in five months, so I don't have that far to go. But the problems continue.

I have lived under bridges and I've lived on the street. I'm at the end of my rope. I have no more family. Death has become acceptable. I have been battling depression and anxiety since 1960. I still have those problems and I also suffer from social phobia. I avoid groups. It is difficult for me to talk to someone even one on one.

Homelessness, living under bridges, panhandling, flying a sign on the highway- it was terrible. I don't think anybody really wants to be there. To experience it. As a matter of fact,

I used to see homeless people and promised myself I would never be that way. I had a home. But here I am.

I am not a healthy person anymore. Homelessness had a lot to do with that. Poor nutrition and poor hygiene. Almost no hygiene. It's just a miserable existence.

At my age I don't know that I have much of a future. I am a solitary person. I isolate a lot. Isolation is my biggest enemy. Well, I'm my biggest enemy, but isolation is a big part. It's a pretty lonely life and like I say, I don't know what the future holds. It is hard for me to accept when people tell me there are still a good ten or fifteen years ahead of me. I don't know if that is true. They can't tell the future any better than I can.

I just want a good, quiet, and peaceful life. I am holding out hope. It is there, but it is not strong at this point. I want to try to stabilize and have a good life. A place to live and take care of myself.

Untitled

By Matt

The world outside of me
Is pleased with itself,
Hiding the horrors and mercies of humanity
I look into the eye of my fellow humans.
And I am filled with despair and hope.
I look into my own eyes,
And see a lost child
With a blank slate to create anything.

By Matt

Arthur

———ᘛᘚ◦ᕔᕀ◦ᕀᕔ◦ᕀ◦ᘛᘚ———

"I never pictured myself here. Never, ever."

I am forty-seven years old. I am a very good father to six beautiful kids. I was hardcore. I was a hard worker. I worked weekends to be able to afford other things. I always made sure my babies had everything. I was a roofer for twenty-three years. I always found a place or a way to work. I was married to the mother of my children for twenty-three years. I never pictured myself here. Never, ever. I lost everything.

I grew up around a lot of drugs. My parents were never there for me. I am barely starting to get involved with them. I was already having my first baby at age sixteen. Throughout my whole life, I have always done a lot for others and never thought about myself. I'd try to make my parents feel happy when instead I should've been out there making myself happy, which I never did.

I was married to this woman for twenty-three years. When I looked at my bank statements there was always money missing. One night I came home drunk and found out that my wife's son was stealing from me and she was lying to me. I beat the shit out of him, so she left me. He was stealing from me and she was letting it go. All he had to do was just talk to me. I could have helped him out.

My kids don't want anything to do with me. I haven't seen them since last year. They just pushed me off. She would always tell my kids bad things about me, always putting me down. What else am I supposed to go out there and do, for them to look at me and call me daddy?

She left me in November. I could have stayed in the house, but there were so many memories. I didn't want to deal with them. I had given a good sum of money to my parents so I decided to go stay with them. I ended up getting into problems with them because they were also stealing from me. Doing the same thing that she was doing. My own parents. I blew up.

I gave up. I quit my job. I tried to commit suicide three times with a gun and twice with a rope. It didn't work. I tried to, I really did. I was at my friend's house. I saw the gun there and I picked it up. I went to where I wanted to pull the trigger, but they walked in at that time. I did this like twice. A lot of them were pissed off at me for doing this. I ended up being referred to a homeless shelter in a large city in the South.

This shelter has helped me a lot. I am getting taken care of here. I never knew that someone could care about a person like me, the way the people here do. The clinician that I see is taking real damn good care of me. She understands where

I come from, maybe because she is Mexican. I am learning how to use coping skills. One of them is journaling. It takes me to another world. It makes me feel different. The more I write, the better I feel. I am here to pick up on things that I did not know about. I am here to pick up on things that they say I have and the medications that I need to take. They say I have Bipolar II. I didn't even know I had it, but they're the doctors.

I go to these classes, and I know that it's not what they can do for me, it's what I can do while they're here: pick up on tips that they throw at you, things you shouldn't forget. The group here, the counselors and the staff, they just want you to go out there and straighten your life out, do things differently.

Every time I get an opportunity to go out there and speak, I am true. I let people know that this can happen to anybody. I tell people to stop taking their life for granted and to keep their heads up because they never know where this life is going to take them. The experience of me being homeless has probably been the worst experience I've ever been through. I was always used to having a house, always used to paying the bills, always looking forward to holidays. I hope to get back to work and get a hold of my kids. I would like to have them there at my house for the holidays or birthdays. I just want to be their father again. I want them at least to hear my side of the story.

Wayne

—⁓∿•⦚⦚•∿⁓—

"We're not thieves or crooks. We're trying. We are trying to get back on our feet."

Being homeless wasn't my choice. I moved down South to start a new life after my divorce. I was coming down here with a friend. He lost his job and was paying for everything until I got a job so I could get out on my own. When he lost his job we came over to the courtyard of this homeless shelter. I stayed there for six months. We came last year in July, but I had to be a county resident in order to move over to the mental health program offered by the homeless shelter. I stayed at the homeless shelter's courtyard for six months, and in July, I started working hard trying to get moved over to the mental health program. I'm finding out a lot of stuff about myself being in this mental health program.

My mind goes blank from time to time. I've been through trauma. At the age of seven, I lost my father. He was killed, murdered. I had a lot of anger when he died. I was also depressed. I ate food to help with my pain and that's how I became overweight. I used to be an athletic person, but I used food for my depression, until I got to my teens. Then I used alcohol. I was drinking way too much.

There's a lot of things that happened in my life. The school counselor said I would never make it out of high school, but I did. I graduated. They said I would never go to college. I did that twice.

I had a girlfriend in high school who was also killed, and that put me through more trauma. I shut myself out, away from other people. Sometimes I think I hold my depression well, until it hits me again. It has been a part of my life. Losing my grandparents was hard, too. My grandfather was a judge. He taught me a lot. He had a lot of wisdom. We both liked to fish and be outdoors. I lived with him until he passed away in 2000. My grandmother passed away in 1995. I took care of both of them. Some grandkids don't do for their grandparents like I did.

I moved back to another city. I started working again at the school district as a dispatcher. I met my wife in 2001, dated her for a while, and married her in 2002. We had three kids. The oldest one, my daughter is ten, the second, my son, is nine. And I have a six-year-old daughter. My wife has mental problems that I thought I dealt with pretty well for a while. Her mom was very controlling. My wife didn't want be around her mom a lot, until we started having our kids. She said she wanted her to see the grandkids. She wanted her mom to see the kids. After I graduated from medical school in 2010, I couldn't find a job, so we had to move in with her.

My wife left for Christmas to go to South America. Her father bought us a house and she wanted to sell that house and bring the money back so we could buy a house in the States. I don't know what happened. When she came back, the kids and I had ended up in a shelter. We were going to counseling and the kids were going to school. I was taking care of them the best I could, but Child Protective Services took the kids away from me and gave them to my wife.

I was in the shelter. I didn't graduate from the program there until the second time. Everything was good. I had a job and went to counseling, stuff like that. When I graduated from that program, I got an apartment. I lived there for about a month or two, maybe three months. Then my friend moved in with me. I was working, but he wasn't. When he landed a job, we moved. When he lost his job, I was homeless again.

A lot has happened while I have been homeless. I've had my phone stolen and an expensive pair of earphones. I made a phonebook with a picture of my kids, but that was stolen. In April of this year there was a death threat put on me. There was a group of us that would sit up at night time to make sure nobody would steal from us. We weren't a gang, but a lot of people thought we were. We were basically a family sticking together, watching after each other. At first I used to sleep in the shelter, but then I moved outside because it was too crowded in there, and that's where a lot of the stuff was happening.

I stayed outside most of the time, all the time to tell the truth. I came down with major depression. That's when I decided to go back to taking medicine. Sometimes that doesn't cure all the stuff that's happened to me. My PTSD started to kick back in. The death threat put on me took me back to my childhood when I had seen my dad's murderers come to our house, and I was freaking out. I was having flashbacks. I couldn't sleep. I sat up in a chair and watched all the walls around. I wasn't sleeping.

Things got worse in August with another death threat. One of the guys that hung around me was sitting in the chair I usually sit in, wearing the same color blue shirt, and he was attacked. That attack was meant for me. That was the word on the street. Right after that happened, I became part of a mental health program at a homeless shelter, for my safety and my personal events.

Throughout my life I have been like a counselor to a lot of the people I have met. That's what I want to do, counsel people. It's in my heart to do that. To help people. I especially want to counsel people who are homeless because I know what it's like to be homeless, and to be depressed.

Homeless people are misrepresented by the way we look, and people look at us in some way like we're crooks, like we're bad people, that we don't have a life. Well, we do have a life. We're not thieves or crooks. We're trying. We are trying to get back on our feet.

My health is my biggest difficulty. I get bad dizzy spells and stuff like that. I want to get my disability and SSI. My main career used to be transportation, but I can't go back to that. My depression is another difficulty. I'm trying. I'm taking it one day at a time. I wake up every morning and thank God. My health is my priority right now, before I can do anything else.

I would like to go back to school to be a counselor and I would like to get my kids back. Going through a divorce and losing my kids is like a death. The holidays suck. I'm not looking forward to Christmas, but I'm planning on leaving here after I get on my feet and do the right things.

I don't want people to become homeless, but if they do there are programs to help you get back on your feet. They help with housing, medication, and health. It's like going on a treasure hunt. The treasure is where everything comes together and you can get on your feet.

I've been sixteen years sober now. I just picture myself at a beach where I can relax.

Amy

*"It's very hard to live with the pain of knowing that
you lost all your children because of being homeless."*

I spent the majority of my life in the South, although
I'm originally from the North, where I was adopted into
a military family. We moved to the Midwest and then to
the South, where my adoptive parents finally settled. I have
a younger biological brother, Tim. He's 31 years old and
currently serving in the military. We were both adopted
by the same family, where we grew up happily. We had an
adoptive sister, Tasha, who was mentally ill, and spent most
of her time in a hospital/nursing home, until her death in
1999. My adopted sister spent most of her time eyes closed,
but when I touched her hand during my visits, she would
open her eyes. That made me feel special.

I talk to my brother every now and then; our relationship
is okay. He's not very happy about the things that I have

done in the past. I used to be into drugs and I had two daughters: Sarah, age 13, and Jane, age 10. I lost custody of both, but I made sure that they remained together. Now I'm trying to better myself by staying here, staying drug free because I have a 7 year-old boy I'm fighting for right now. His name is Max. He is currently in foster care.

I was actually doing very well. I had my own place and CPS just came by and took him from me, without even giving me a drug test. My neighbor across the street at the time called CPS on me because I was supposedly buying drugs from her, but I was clean at the time.

I was adopted when I was 2 years old. I really don't know much about my biological mother, but I would love to find out more and find her. My adoptive mother knows about my biological mother, but she will not tell me because she thinks that I would stop loving her. I do know that I look like my mother, according to my stepmother, and that we were removed from my mother's care. I'm hoping this book will help me find her.

I was very happy with my adoptive mother and father. I was especially close to my adoptive father, but they divorced and my adoptive father moved away. Actually, prior to the divorce, my adoptive father was angry all the time. Then, when my adoptive father left, my stepfather came into the picture right away, and I didn't really like him, I didn't like that my adoptive mother moved so fast. My stepfather would treat us very nice in the beginning, my brother and I, but then his true colors came out over the years. The reason I became homeless is because of him. My adoptive mother and I did not get along like I did with my adoptive father, and he kept telling my mom, "If she's going to live here, then I'm leaving." So I left.

I became homeless since I left my home at 21 years old and I was still in high school. I was in special education classes. I did not give up on high school; I spent some nights at my friend's house, night after night, until I graduated high school. When I graduated, I ended up at a homeless shelter where I met a guy, Carl, and I had my first daughter with him. I was 22 years old by this time and we ended up together - I left the shelter to be with him. Carl and I did not work out; we were only together for about 2 years. I started using drugs right after I graduated high school. Carl is the one that got me into drugs. After Carl, I met John, and we had a baby together, my daughter Jane, who is 10 years old now.

When I was with Carl, I fell in love with his friend Bryan. When I first met Bryan, I thought he was just so adorable, like when you just see like a glow. That's my son's dad. And still today I love that man. Bryan is currently incarcerated due to a third DWI. Bryan does not use drugs; he just has a drinking problem. That's it.

I have no contact with Carl, but I do have some contact with John who is currently incarcerated as well. I just received a letter from him yesterday and he appears to be doing well. But the one that I do want to keep in touch with is my son's dad, Bryan. Bryan is the love of my life. Since he's been in there for two years, I think he's learned his lesson. He's aware that his son is in foster care, and he tells me that I am a good mom for fighting for our son. He's very proud of me. He keeps telling me that I'm a beautiful mom and to keep my head up and that everything will be good. I'm the one that has been fighting for him for three years and two months and I still haven't given up.

I was diagnosed with Schizophrenia/Bipolar/Depression/Anxiety, ADD and I have asthma. I was also born with hip dysplasia. I believe that my mental illnesses played a part in losing my children, as well as the substance abuse. Also, what I went through as a kid, because my stepfather, he was very abusive with my brother and I. My stepfather was very mean. My brother and I used to have braces and he would squeeze our gums into our braces really hard, which was very painful. Once he was teaching me how to ride the lawn mower and I thought I was doing it right, but he got mad at me and yanked me off of it and then I kept seeing the lawn mower going by itself. He then kept telling me, "If you don't catch it, your ass is grass." He would make me write lines all the time for anything that I did wrong. My adoptive father left when I was 10 years old, so I went through that abuse for a long time.

I still have contact with my adoptive mom and right now it's good. My stepfather and I have a better relationship now, but I only really visit my adoptive mother now. I really don't care to see him.

One of my most memorable childhood experiences was when my brother and I would play out in the snow up North. We would have our snow suits on. We would jump from our balcony onto the snow and that is when my brother and I were really close. When we were growing up, we were very close, but now that we are older, we're not that close anymore. He has two beautiful daughters, Erica and Mary.

I think that I have some family support with my adoptive mother, but I'm here at the shelter because I really want to find my real mom. My adoptive mother told me that my real family was incestuous, and that they live in the North. I have asked my adoptive mother for information about my real mother but she is afraid that I am going to look up my real mom and forget about her. But I am not going to forget about my adoptive mom, she took care of me, but I really, really want to know about my real mom. My brother does not really care about our real mom.

I write poems and listen to music when I want to relax. And I create my own music. I love to play the drums. I love to go to church, it is my favorite thing. I like to read my bible. I love to look at pictures of my son, pictures of my son's dad. I just imagine them being together playing. He was a very good father. When they took my son, we were all together. We just looked at each other and I just begged him not to leave me.

When I lost my son Max, I was very depressed all the time. I couldn't eat, couldn't sleep. But I've learned to cope with it, because after seeing him in visitations, it gives me strength to keep fighting for him. Bryan is also a source of inspiration to keep working hard for our son. He is the love of my life.

There were so many times that I wanted to do ice, my drug of choice, but Bryan kept me from using. When we were all still together and Bryan would hold Max and then tell me: "Here, you know what to do if you want us in your life." And I would flush the drugs down the toilet. I have been clean since 2006.

I was sleeping outside the shelter for 3 months before transitioning to a program for people who are homeless and with a mental health illness. Prior to coming to the program

I was at different shelters. I have always been homeless, since my adoptive mother, at the request of my stepfather, kicked me out of my adoptive home. I had both of my daughters while being homeless. I had Max with me when I was in the battered women's shelter due to domestic violence in a relationship with another man.

Sometimes, being homeless happens because you don't have the love that kids are supposed to get from their parents. When you are feeling this pain, the only things that will make the pain go away are drugs because you don't know any other way. Drugs don't really take the pain, though. The worst part about being homeless for me now is not having my son with me because I am homeless. It's very hard to live with the pain of knowing that you lost all your children because of being homeless. My medical problem, the hip dysplasia, makes it difficult for me to work. And not having a steady income keeps me from having a stable place to live. Also, my mental health problems make it difficult for me to keep a job. If somebody yells at me, I'm going to yell back. It's very difficult for me to control myself.

My dreams are to have a place of my own one-day, after I finish my program and become eligible for a place. I'm hoping that I can get my son back and eventually get together with my son's father.

Jared

"I'm lil JC chilling here at the ranch, going to make my momma proud and make her dance."

My name is Jared. I was born in 1995 in the Eastern US. I am 19 years old and I am diagnosed with Bipolar disorder. That's why I am in this shelter.

I have had some good times in my life and others, not so good.

My birth mother didn't want me in her life, so she put me up for adoption when I was 10 months old. I never saw her again. I was adopted by a woman named Amy. She has been by my side since. My mother was in the military for 22 years before she retired in 2009. Since she was in the military, we moved around a lot. I've lived in different US states and overseas. Growing up I remember hanging out with my little brothers Rudy and Brandon when my mom was at work. Some of the things I remember the most are snowboarding and going to indoor pools in the Western US and playing in the haystacks with my brothers overseas.

Not everything was good though. One night, when I was 5 years old, my mom was called off to go to work. She left me with my dad and told me I could go to sleep in their room if I was scared of the dark. So, I went to my dad to see if I could sleep there, and he let me sleep on the floor. In the middle of the night I happened to wet my pants. My dad wasn't very happy about that. I saw him go into the closet and come out with some shoe laces. He tied my wrists and ankles together and went to the kitchen to boil some water. While the water was boiling he turned on the hot water to fill the tub. He went back to get the water and poured it in the bath tub. He stuck my arms in there and burned them. My arms have been burned since. The doctors even had to cut off my left ring finger because they couldn't save it. My dad went to jail, and we ended up moving in order to get away from him.

Soon enough, I started noticing myself getting angry at little things. For example, one Christmas, when I was about 9 years old, I broke my brand new gaming system my mom had just bought for me. I couldn't beat the game, so I hit it with my head and broke it. I was about 13 when my bipolar really started getting out of hand. We were living in out of the US at the time. I began to be mean to my family. I would yell at my mom and tell her I didn't like her along with other horrible things. My mom decided I needed to get some help. So, she sent me to a boys' ranch out West.

At the boys' ranch, they tried to help me get better. I made a few friends there. My mom would visit me from time to time. On one of her trips to see me I handed her a CD with a song I had made for her. The song was called "There's a Better Way, Better Day." Some of the lyrics read: "I'm lil JC chilling here at the ranch, going to make my momma proud and make her dance, put your hands up high, wave them side to side. JC in the house so it's time to ride. There's a better way, better day if I try a little harder in this life to do what's right." I stayed there for a few months. After my days were up I went back overseas with my family.

I was only with my family for a few months before my bipolar started getting out of hand again. My mom knew I still needed help. I wanted help too. I wanted to change. I wanted to be better. My mom found a psychiatric facility in the South. My mom and I got on a plane and flew over there. I told my mom I loved her and promised her I was going to change and get better.

A few months later I was out of the psychiatric facility. My family had moved to be near to me. When I saw our new home, I was surprised. It was the most beautiful home I had ever seen. I soon enrolled at a local high school to begin my freshman year of high school and then transferred in 12th grade to a different high school in the same city. I had a few episodes in the following years where I had to go back to the psychiatric facility for a couple of weeks each time. I graduated high school in June 2013, and I remember going to dinner at a family restaurant. I was proud of having graduated high school. I was happy I got a high school diploma and not a GED.

Five months after my graduation I got my first criminal charge. The bipolar was back. I was throwing rocks at random cars and got caught. I was arrested and spent a night in jail. Weeks after that, I stole a tip jar from a donut shop.

I was arrested and spent 4 months in jail. I was connected with the case management resources once I was released from jail.

I got out of jail and went back home for a little while, before things got bad again. My mom sent me to a boarding home. I was there for a few weeks and then I got in trouble and got kicked out for supposedly stealing some pills, which I didn't do. I was transferred to another boarding home. I got kicked out of that place too for fighting with someone who was talking about my momma. My caseworker took me to a crisis unit, where I stayed for only 2 weeks. I told my caseworker I wanted to be a part of this program at the shelter. He told me that the only way to get there was to go back to a boarding home. I went back and that same night I got out of control. I missed my mom so much that I started hitting myself and punching myself. The police were called, and I was kicked out again.

The only place I could go was outside of the shelter. During intake I met this man that I didn't know. He said he wanted to hang out with me and invited me to a hotel. I immediately told him I didn't roll like that. He insisted so I finally went with him and his friend. I was completely uncomfortable not knowing what he was going to do. Once we were in the room he told me to take off my shirt. I said no, so he slapped me and punched me. I tried to run out the door, but he pushed me back. I started banging on the door, and the neighbor finally came. He knocked on the room door and when this man opened it I screamed and let him know that this man was trying to rape me. I ran as far as I could. I called the police and pressed charges on him. After that I called my caseworker and luckily, he let me know that they had a room ready for me in the shelter.

I have been here since June 25, and it has helped me out a lot. When I get out of here I plan on going back home and be with my family. I come from a good family. I love my mom and my brothers. They have been a great support and have been helping me get better. The reason why I am here is because of my bipolar. I have been on medications all of my life, but I am learning how to live with it. It is not fun being here, but I know it's for my own good. I just want to make my mom proud.

By Jared

Elva

"I've noticed that people look down at us. I don't understand. We do everything we can to be somebody, to be something."

Sometimes a parent listens to their children a little bit more than they should. I listened to one of my children a little bit more than I should; he convinced me to put all my stuff in pawn shops. So I did. So I put all my stuff in pawn shops, and he said he was going to take 'em all out, and he said he was going to pay half of the rent. So I said, "Okay, that's awesome. You gonna help me out." But at the beginning of the month he left all my stuff in the pawn shop and he doesn't pay his share of the rent; he takes off. So I am literally left in the dark with no money. I just have my half of the rent. So I went to go talk to the manager, to see if we could make an arrangement. I told her, "You know what? I can get a job. I can get a part time job and I can

126

get you the first couple of checks; I could just pass them to you, no problem." She said, "No. I want the money now." So I said, "Okay, do what you gotta do." So, she proceeded to evict me.

I had to move everything into storage. I had one storage, and I still had a lot of furniture, but I didn't have money. My neighbor asked if she could help, so she kept a lot of my big furniture. I didn't have anywhere else to go; so me and my daughter slept under the bridge and we stayed there that night with my dog. When we came to the shelter they took us in. I couldn't sleep on the floor because of my back problems, diabetes, and all that stuff, so the shelter took me in right away. But they said that the only way they would take us in is if I let my dog be adopted. This was hard because we had had our puppy for about 4 months and he had already grown big time. My daughter was heartbroken, but I looked at her and said, "Baby, I can't make it on the street no more. I can't do it, my body won't let me."

My daughter was 21 and we'd never been homeless before. I've always been able to have my job and be able to hold a job, but I just became ill and I wasn't able to maintain. I was a security guard and I liked it. When I was 45 I got hurt at work. I remember I had to go to the medical clinic and all kinds of things are going on! They told me not to go to work and then they started sending me my checks. I was getting disability, but $730 just doesn't go very far per month for three people. I would go to the thrift stores and garage sales to get my kids clothes and stuff, but it's impossible.

Before this, when my kids were younger, they would get mad at me having to leave them all the time. I told them that if I didn't work we wouldn't have an apartment to live in. If I didn't work we wouldn't have food. I had to do something in order for us to have a house and electricity and water and food. The kids would look at me and they would be angry with me and be hating me a lot. Sometimes they wouldn't talk to me for days; even on my days off sometimes they wouldn't talk to me. It's okay. I understood. I understood why they were angry. There was nothing I could do about it; I had to work.

Now that they are older they have turned around and said that they understand. It took them a while. There were a lot of things that happened that I wasn't aware of. When my son was 10 and my daughter was 9, I found out that my husband was abusing my kids. That is when it all started. I kicked him out.

We stayed at the house for a while, till I noticed that he was driving by a lot and I was worried that he would take my little kids, my two little ones, because they were his. So we started moving to apartment to apartment so he wouldn't find us. Then he took off. He wasn't paying child support, so he shouldn't have the right to see his kids. They were MY kids, not his.

He had hit me too. More than once; he hit me three times. After the third hit I started hitting back. I'm bi-polar, so I hit and I wouldn't stop hitting.

When I first became homeless, I felt sad. I felt like I had failed my daughter, as a mother. I couldn't sleep good... we slept under the bridge. There were two spots and I made sure my daughter slept on the inside so in case some guy came he would have to hit me first instead of my daughter. I always protected my daughter. My puppy, I put her next to me by my feet. I kept watching her to make sure she was okay. I didn't want anything to happen to her either. I kept watch over both of them most of the night. My eyes were burning the next day, cause of the dust under us. The next day my body hurt! I am diabetic and I have arthritis all over my body. I was in pain and I told my daughter that I couldn't do it. I said, "I love you, but I can't do it."

My daughter had found some information about this shelter. She figured they would let me in because of my health problems and we hoped they would let her in too. I remember when I came to the shelter I told them that if I came in I wouldn't do it if they wouldn't let my daughter come in. I said, "If you don't let my daughter in then the deal's off." She HAD to come in with me. They let her in a different program, but I know she is just across the way from me. I know she is safe, I know she will be okay. She will have a roof over her head.

I was hurt because I had to give the puppy away. That hurt us BIG time because we had promised not to give her away. But we didn't know it would get so bad so fast; we thought we could handle staying with her. We just miscalculated. That was all. For a long time I was numb while I was in here.

I don't want to stay any longer than I have to. That's just me, that's my thing. Some people, you know people, they give me a hard time because I get up every morning or night and when I have the energy I still iron my clothes. They say, "Why do you iron your clothes? You live at a shelter! You know you're homeless?" "Yeah," I say, "but just because you are homeless don't mean you have to look like shit."

I like to look good for myself. If I don't look good, I feel like I DO feel homeless; REALLY homeless. That is when I feel like I don't want to live. When you see me with my clothes not ironed those are the days I feel like I don't want to live. I just don't care whether I live or die then. When the kids see me without ironed clothes, they know how I feel. They know things. They ask what is wrong. I reply, "You don't want to know. You don't want to know what I feel right now. Just leave me alone. Just leave me alone." I'll live, just because I have to, not because I want to. That is why I am still around.

My kids are my life. I love my family. That is why I am around. I am around, and I am doing all this process, I am going through all this process.

I hope to get an apartment. I hope that eventually my oldest daughter overlooks my disabilities and allows me to see my grandchild, but I'm not going to hold my breath. I will give her my address once I move, and I will tell her this is my address and if she wants she can bring the baby around. If she chooses not to, then I understand, too. But I want to make sure my grandbaby knows it was her parent's choice, and not mine. If given the opportunity to see her, I would see her in a heartbeat.

I want people to know that people don't choose to be homeless. People don't know from one day to another if they are going to be homeless. And don't look down on homeless people, we are people, too. People seem to judge us so swiftly and meanly and it hurts sometimes. We don't have a disease! We are not infected! We are just people too. We just want a chance at life just like everyone else does. We just had bad luck. Who is to say that they are not going to get bad luck at one time or another? Or that their families are going to get bad luck? Nobody knows, it's not written in a book. Hope to God that this doesn't happen but nobody knows. So why judge? Why judge anybody? We are all humans, we all bleed the same.

It is not right what people do sometimes. I have noticed it, people treat us differently. I've noticed that people judge us. I've noticed that people look down at us. I don't understand. Do we smell? We all take showers! We love ourselves, you know? We take care of ourselves. We do everything we can to be somebody, to be something. We wake up in the morning wanting to go out there and join the world; get jobs, become somebody important. Not to be ignored, not to be looked down at; to be a part of life. People shouldn't look down on us. If you can't love us, just let us be. If you can't say something good about us, just leave us alone.

Kyle

—⁓ↄⲟⲉⲧⲟⲟⲧⲉ⳽ⲟⲟⲙ—

*"I was supposed to be a father, work one job my
entire life, come home every day and raise my kids. It
didn't happen that a way."*

I'm 51 years old. I've learned something every day of my
life, but it hasn't been a cake walk. It's no Bill Gates story.
It's hard, real hard.

I came to the shelter in the first place because probation sent
me. I was on federal probation for three years, and I violated
it and was sent back to the penitentiary. I did my prison time
in a town where don't have a program like this, so I came here.
When I was released from the penitentiary, my probation
officer sent me here under a mandatory type deal. I was
on medication in the penitentiary. After penitentiary you
have to do some half-way house or something. The half-
way house doesn't accept people on meds so I came here.
Since I was 22 I've had a diagnosis. It's been progressive.

Tis

By Emily aka "Leah"

Tis in life
As in a picture
There's more to it
Than we may see
But then again
What is not is
And what is, is not
Tis…

That's about where my problems started. I lost my family. I got married at a very young age, 17. I had my very first child. And I had a grand design for my life of who I wanted to be. I've never been really happy with who I turned out to be. I've had great success and I've been homeless several times. Multiple stays in hospitals and things like that. My diagnosis went from Depression to Major Depression to Bipolar, Bipolar II. In 2000, when I was working, I was involved in a fatal accident. A lady lost her life. I was a truck driver – it's what I did. After that I was working the whole time trying to get through these court proceedings and things 'cause the family sued my company. Then I had my first experience with delusions, audible, visual. I was working on the road and doing all this in the truck, experiencing this from the road, and having to deal with my job. I owned a company at the time, but I just couldn't handle it anymore. It got bad.

I stopped in the Midwest to get fuel. It took like 30 minutes to fill the truck up. So there's two trucks ahead of me. So I go inside to make a call, I have an argument with my dispatcher girlfriend, and I go out and get into the truck and take off without even getting fuel. About 90 miles down the road I ran out of fuel right in the middle of the freeway. I just got out of the truck and started walking back the other way. Somebody picked me up and took me to a psychiatric center. I spent 45 days there with a diagnosis of Schizoaffective (disorder). They turned me loose, bought me a plane ticket home, told me not to ever work again. I went back and worked an additional 11 years. I've never really had a home. I was homeless in the truck a few times. I had jobs and I lived in the truck. I raised my kids and I paid my child support. The times that I did have to be out looking and living under the bridge or whatever, I worked real hard. I hated that life. I hated that feeling. You just don't know the feeling 'til you walk into a store, you know, and all eyes are on you, like you're some kind of disease or something. And I really hated that feeling so I really tried hard not to be homeless.

I've been homeless in different states. I read the Bible several times. I studied the Bible several times. I've lived under the bridge with the Bible as my pillow. So I relate it to the experiences that Jesus had. You eat whatever's given. It's your walk. So if I say walk, it's what I mean, it's my plight, it's how I ended up. I was supposed to be a father, work one job my entire life, come home every day and raise my kids. It didn't happen that a way. I lost everything I ever loved. I've been so down that not even a slightest little dream can come true.

I got better up to my stay in the state hospital, after prison. I stayed seven months because I had to go somewhere. I finally found a doctor and a team that took their time. Seven months is a long stay in a mental hospital. They took the time and got that medicine just right, and I started using all the years of therapy and stuff. I started recognizing when I was having delusions. No medicine ever took the voices away.

I hung myself in jail, but the rope broke. I tried to step out in front of a truck and tripped over my laces and fell in the rocks. I can't do it, I have done more dope than would kill an elephant and lived through it. I had two brothers that died at an early age, one at 22 and one at 45. My two older brothers died from doing drugs; I can't do it. There's no way I can take my own life, I got to see it through. That's my plight.

My depression is a major challenge in my experience of homelessness. When you are homeless, you just don't have anywhere to go. You don't have anything to do. Being a truck driver is a lot like being homeless. Your job is to sit there and hold the wheel, and run through the gears, twenty million times a day. So you have a lot of time to think, sooner or later you learn all the words to every song on the radio. It's a lot like homelessness. You just sit there on the sun or on the rock and you wait, you wait, you wait. It's a big waiting game.

When you're a kid you got your plan. When you finish school you're going to be great at what you do. This is what you want. This is what you're trying for. What if that was taken from you? What would you do? If your dream was taken. I don't know. I don't know how to answer that. It hurts. I got through the depression by just pushing. Perseverance man.

I was homeless in the South. I was using a Nelson Study Bible as my pillow, everything I owned in my bag. I started my journey. There's a truck stop there. I started walking, carrying that big ol' bag on my back. This was August in the South, it's very hot. It took me three days to walk 36 miles because you can't hitch hike there. I was sleeping in the ditches with my Bible as my pillow. I was reading. I'd walk until I couldn't and I'd drink water people would give me. I finally made it there. I got on the CB, I asked for a ride to a town a few hours away.

I got a ride with a truck driver going to the state capital. He let me there. I stayed the night with my Bible as my pillow. I got up the next morning. I settled on a truck with a Mexican driver. He pulled in there and gave me a ride. I said I was a truck driver. I had a CDL. He said "Well, I'll get you a job." I was waiting for the application to process, which I figured it wouldn't 'cause I'd left a truck in the middle of the road in another state. I figured my driving career was over. So the three days I was waiting on a word on the application with the truck driving company, I stayed in a drivers' room at a truck stop in another metropolitan city. At night I'd go across, there was a big sign on the ground, and I'd sleep in the grass behind the sign. I took my wallet out, put it in my shoes, put my shoes under my head, and fell asleep. Someone stole my shoes with my wallet in it that night.

So there I was homeless, no shoes, no job. I walked across the freeway to the a truck stop, used the pay phone, called the truck driving company and they said, "You're accepted, we have a bus ticket waiting for you at such and such place, here's the confirmation number." I wrote the confirmation number down, I went out on a fuel line. I ask a driver which way he was headed, he said south. He bought me a pair of shoes, gave me $25 for a driver's license. I went to the bus station, got on a bus, went to a large Midwest city, did the orientation, worked 17 years for that trucking company. So it was hell getting there, but when I finally got there, it was a blessing. My mental health has probably played a role in all of my experience of homelessness. I couldn't wait to get out of my parents' house. I couldn't wait to get out of there. I just had to get my life started. And I was listening to my voice. And I didn't recognize it back then. I married the wrong woman, just a lot of things – a lot of things went wrong. Rising out of homelessness is difficult. I got older, my health is failing. I'm a bad diabetic, insulin dependent, and so I have to have a refrigerator for the insulin. Seeing as how I worked most of my life, I don't get all the freebies. The free medicine, the free this, that. I have to pay. But I make more money than just regular people. I don't know. There's always going to be stumbling blocks for me. It's never going to be easy. It's never going to be what I want it to be. It's gonna be what was put on the table for me. I wish the two would align somewhere down the road. I believe that's true peace.

You find peace in your life. And I have experienced peace, God's peace.

I do still have dreams. And I do have hopes for the future. My family, that's a heartache for me. I missed everything, but I do not owe a dime. Child support sent me money back when my daughter aged out. I'm proud of that part, but I missed everything. Holidays. I want 'em all to be in one state, possibly even the same city. If they all moved here, I could die tomorrow a happy man. But just within one state where they could drive, and we could do holidays, all together, as a family. That's my hope. I think the world takes you down to a place where you have to learn. You have to see that stealing's wrong, lying is not right. Some people just don't ever get it. Some die, and changing the way they feel, that's the deal. Nobody can handle the feeling of being there, in that place.

Emily aka "Leah"

"Life is hard just to be a 'normal' person. It can be real challenging if you have a mental illness."

Some of the things that have happened in my life are due to me making bad choices, but other things that have happened to me are just life. Life just happens. There is both of that in my story.

I went from my daddy, to my first husband, which was a 25-year marriage with 5 children, to my second relationship, which was with Bobby. I didn't know how to support myself. I had gone from my dad, to my husband, to Bobby. Codependency is a part of my story. One of the things we learn in the women's program is identifying what codependency is. None of us are really independent. We are all dependent on each other, but we are learning in the program how to become interdependent. If we are in a relationship and we break up or something happens to you, I will still be ok.

I came from a really good family. However, all of my immediate family has passed away now. My parents were from the North and they moved to the South when my daddy got into the oil and gas refine products, like gasoline service stations and so forth. My mother was a full-time housewife.

They called me their dessert. I was their third child, and my brothers were in their twenties when I was born. My dad was well off financially. We lived an upper-middle class lifestyle until around 1970. My older brother, Paul, was overseas and an alcoholic, big-time. My brother Luke was a student at a university. He overdosed on heroin, but my parents hadn't even known he was on drugs. That same month my mother was diagnosed with emphysema and that's when my life kind of turned upside down.

For the next ten years my mother was in and out of hospitals with respiratory failure. We had nursed her and because of her illness we had nurses in our home around the clock.

My parents had moved us to get me away from the drugs. They were scared after they lost Luke. I still got involved with drugs. I remember when I was thirteen I had a boyfriend, and he turned me on to drugs for the first time. I remember thinking, "Oh, well, this takes all the pain away." I don't think I ever used recreationally. I think I always used as an addict. I used to change the way I felt.

My parents were functioning alcoholics – my dad never missed work. He always provided a home, but my mother was on a lot of medications and she did drink. I witnessed a lot of passing out, falling out at the table. I was always worried about them. My drug addiction started when I was thirteen years old and lasted until I was twenty seven, pretty hard core.

Mark, my first husband, and I were married for twenty plus years. We fell in love while we were in our addiction, when I was 25, but we stopped when we got pregnant. I was 27.

After my first son was born, my brother Paul lived with my husband and me. He had been in jail on alcohol related charges, and my dad and I bonded him out. Once, in the middle of the night, he took off on my mother-in-law's motorcycle. He was drunk and he hydroplaned. He hit his head three times and he landed in fire ants. The fire ants' poison killed him.

After that I had ten years of sobriety and at that point we had five children. My dad used to say they were nine months and five minutes apart – we had so many.

This is what happened – I had ten years sober, my dad was living with us, and we had a home. We had a mortgage, car payments, life insurance. I was the minivan mom. I was a full-time mom. Five kids is a lot. I was breastfeeding. My kids went to dance, soccer, karate. My son was in private golf lessons. We did gymnastics and swimming lessons. That's what I did. But I had disconnected myself from my programs in AA and NA. I was still on my meds, but then my dad was diagnosed with terminal cancer. I remember my first thought was, "Well a glass of wine would calm my nerves."

We had health insurance. I could have seen a psychiatrist or gone to an AA meeting. But the disease of addiction is progressive, chronic, and incurable. We don't graduate. You have to stay connected, because the disease lives in your mind. It can tell you that you're healed or that you're ok or that you can drink again. That weekend I thought that, and I chose to drink.

In nine months I was full blown into my addiction. Mark had gotten into his addiction again. We got pulled over and got a possession charge. We had drugs in the car, and the kids were in the car, so they took them into care. They were with my mother-in-law for a while, but she wasn't appropriate. They put them in foster care. They were adopted into a home.

Before he died my dad told me, "I left money to the children in trusts. I know you and your addiction. Once I die I'm afraid you'll kill yourself because of the drugs. I left the money to the children, but I love you and you are a great mother to my grandbabies."

When Mark and I divorced, I crashed, just like I did when my dad and my mom died.

I first met Bobby when we were both homeless, living under the bridge. I had been working for two different companies while living at a shelter following my divorce. I was kicked out of the shelter when I came up dirty for smoking weed, and I was unable to keep up with the two jobs. So I had been sleeping outside, under a bridge when I met Bobby.

Bobby was very abusive, but I knew how to be submissive in the relationship so that I didn't get my assed kicked. I was not allowed to ever go without a bra, I could not wear shorts, I couldn't wear skirts above my knee, and I wasn't allowed to wear makeup. I wasn't allowed to eat chicken. I was only allowed to eat dark meat, because that is what he liked. But he was my provider. He provided my home.

One night we got separated. When I came back he was so irate that he didn't know where I had been. He beat me down to the ground, kicking my head, kicking me in the ribs. He yelled, "Bitch, why don't you fight to protect yourself? I'm going to smash your head in with this!" He picked up this big rock. "I'm going to smash your head in."

I looked at him and said, "Please don't kill me. I want to see my children again."

He snapped and he didn't hit me with that rock. I knew Bobby was abusive, but he protected me from all of the other chaos and drama going on in homelessness. So I stayed with him. We were together about ten years, and had a home for about seven of those.

About five years into the relationship I got pregnant with Rebecca. We had this beautiful little girl. I was a stay at home mom, but I wasn't living my true self. I was Bobby's girl. That's what everyone called me. "Bobby's girl." A lot of people didn't even know my name. I was just Bobby's girl. We were living in a little town house. I stayed home with Rebecca and Bobby provided our living. Then I got a call from my oldest son, John, who was eighteen. "Mom, I want to see you."

I had four years of sobriety, but my life started to cycle back out of control again.

When my son came back, instead of it being the homecoming that I had waited for and dreamed of, it was a problem because Bobby was jealous of John. He was jealous of the attention that I gave John and he accused me of being with John's father. I was getting hit in front of my children.

At one point we got in such a fight that I kicked him out after he hit me so hard. Then I caught him with another woman. He was drinking again. It was just out of control.

I got off of all my meds, and I went into a serious depression. Whenever I get off of my meds, I get severely depressed, I can hardly get out of bed. I had caught Bobby with another woman and my reunion with my kids was just a mess.

One day Bobby came to visit Rebecca. We were arguing and he said that on Friday he wasn't going to come and bring the check. He was just being a butt, but I panicked. I was off my meds, and I had become suicidal. I said, "Oh, really? Well, watch this!" I took a glass, broke it, and cut myself on my left wrist. I didn't mean to kill myself. I was trying to get his attention. "Hey, I need help!" "I'm desperate!" "I don't feel good. Help, help, help, help!" It was a cry for help.

I was in the bathtub and he was freaking out thinking I was trying to bleed out to die. I told him, "I'm going to the hospital. Don't call the police because if you call the police then they are going to get CPS involved with Rebecca."

He called EMS and they came. I went to the hospital. It was deep. I had nineteen staples. Three days later there was a knock at the door. It was the police and CPS.

They checked the refrigerator first. But we had plenty of food. We had a beautiful house. But I had this cut, so they were going to take Rebecca from me. They opened a CPS case, and Bobby had been smoking weed and drinking, so they removed Rebecca from our home. We got into another fight and he gave me another black eye and busted my nose all up. This time I pressed charges, and I went to a women's shelter.

The old patterns of behavior came back, and I didn't know how to take care of myself, so I decided the easiest way to get Rebecca back would be if Bobby and I get sober and get back together. So that's what we did. Nine months later we got her back.

At this point my two oldest daughters, who were eighteen and seventeen, came to live with us. I had grounded my daughter for skipping school. One night she didn't come home from school, so I sent my other daughter to get her. When she came in she was so mad. She came in and said, "Bobby has been coming on to me sexually."

I went into a rage. I didn't know who to trust. Who to believe or what to do. I called CPS and told them. They told me, "Don't use, keep taking your medicine. If you can't keep the apartment, go to a women's shelter and we will support you so you don't lose Rebecca."

I was in so much pain. Emotional pain and spiritual pain. I used.

I lost Rebecca again. I tried to fight to get her back, but CPS wanted to close the case. They did not take my rights, but asked me to find an appropriate family member to take Rebecca until I could get on my feet. I didn't have any immediate family alive and my older children were just graduating high school and getting into college. They couldn't take care of a child. I asked Bobby's sister who lived in the South. We put Rebecca on a plane and sent her to her aunt.

That's when I went into the depths.

I stopped taking my meds. I didn't care anymore. I got into my addiction. I used cocaine and alcohol. The women on the street taught me prostitution. That's where I got

145

"Leah," my street name. I did that for three years. I got one prostitution case and I was caught stealing food at a store for myself. I was put on four years' probation.

I thought I was going to prison. I was scared. I was totally sick on my addiction. I was off my meds. I was starting to hallucinate. I ended up going to the shelter where they have a program which connects you to resources. They got me back on meds and got me a probation advocate who is really supportive.

"Leah" is dead now. I can integrate some of Leah into me because she was a survivor and she was strong, but I don't ever want to have to live that life again. That was a horrible way to live.

Now I am in the women's program. It has three phases. The first two are intensive groups with three to four groups a day, and we talk about relationships, codependency, setting boundaries, and medication information. Here I can adjust my meds and make sure things are right before I get back out on my own.

I have had several relapses since I came here. I was scared to death. We had been revisiting the trauma in my life and I was triggered by that. I broke down and they got me to the hospital. They opened my eyes that I'm still worthy and that somebody still believes in me. I didn't have to beat myself up this time. Sometimes relapse is part of recovery.

Not all people have to go through it, but some people do. It doesn't mean that you deserve to be locked up with violent people. I can be abusive to myself, but I'm not a danger to other people. I'm now in stage three where we're working on finding a job and housing. I don't know how long it is going to take, but I am going to take my time. I don't know that I am ready to be on my own.

I communicate a lot with Rebecca. I talk to her on the phone any time I want. I know I am a good mother because I'm not the kind of mom that's going to say "That's my baby and I want my baby back. Mine, mine, mine, mine!" No. She's a child of God and God gave me a chance and I fell short. She's somewhere where she is stable and she's excelling in school. She's in the church and she sings. I want to get healthy and well, so I can be an addition to her life. Where I can come get her in the summer and have her for a few weeks. Possibly, maybe someday I'll move close to her where I can attend her church. But I'm not on the bandwagon to get my daughter back because I think that would be totally selfish. She's happy and she's stable, and I don't want to put her through any more than she's already been through. That would be selfish.

My voice, when I get well enough, will be to women with children that are in addiction, mental illness, and so forth. I would tell them to consider adoption; to love unselfishly enough to let go so the babies can have a stress free, stable home. Consider adoption, consider asking for help.

Sarah is my second oldest. She is in college and wants to be a veterinarian. She makes really good grades. John and Sarah love me and we have conversations. Not a lot, but we're in touch. We see each other from time to time.

Heather, my third child says I disgust her. She's got a lot of anger and she's got a right to her anger. I just opened a new Facebook account and friend requested her. She accepted it, so that tells me she still wants to talk. She wants me to be able to follow her, but her words would tell you she never wants to see me again. The last time I talked to her was on her birthday. I let her know that anything she needs to say to me she can say and I'm going to listen. I will listen to her, but I also have to forgive myself. I can't beat myself up forever.

Sally is the fourth, and I don't have any contact with her. She's living with her dad right now. It's a little overwhelming to me. Jeff, the youngest, is still in the adoptive home.

I have bipolar disorder, Post-Traumatic Stress Disorder, and anxiety disorder. I am considered high functioning, but my mental illness plays a large role. I don't know how many times in the past I decided "I'm good, I don't need my medication," and I crashed.

I had a job at a restaurant and they put me on the morning shift. It was high paced and I kept messing up and messing up and messing up. My boss noticed, and he knew I had this disability, but that's when he witnessed what goes on with me and he's like, "Now I see." He put me on the swing shift so I could manage, but I didn't make much money. I got overwhelmed real easily.

I'm in a relationship now with a man who doesn't understand mental illness. It's difficult because he thinks, "Well, what do you need these meds for?" I've had too many setbacks for me to buy into that lie.

Life is hard just to be a "normal" person. It can be real challenging if you have a mental illness. I don't hear voices or see things, but my depression can get to the point where I just can hardly get out of bed. It's like having a heavy backpack full of bricks on your back and walking around with that. I've tried several jobs, but it was extremely hard for me to function.

Being homeless is like being in a hole and there's no ladder and no stairs. You're looking up and you can't get back up and out. Once you're homeless it is hard to find a job. My biggest challenge right now is being able to find housing. When Bobby and I separated two times, my name was on the lease, so I have two evictions on my record and the theft charge. People are not going to want to rent to me. I don't want to move back into a neighborhood that's infested with drug addiction and crime because those are triggers for me in my recovery. Also, I can never get food stamps again because of my possession charge from so long ago when I was with Mark.

I'd like to maybe get back into college. I'm college eligible. I was in college during four years of sobriety, so I know I can pass. Maybe some substance abuse counseling or something like that would be a way to live in recovery and help someone else. And I've always been interested in culinary. I just want to have a simple life. I just want to stay sober. I want to have a nice home for my grandchildren to visit me if they want to.

This Program Helps

By Mari

Understanding mental disorders, is hard for
those whom believe they are sane.
The lack of compassion, and empathy, causes us to rage.
So, many other have treated it like it's a
game. To lay around in luxury, using money
slated for us to feel partially sane.

The game which was played by the posers,
backfired in their faces. Meds which they did
not need, change their games into reality.
Now, the doors to help are harder to open, due
to the falsehood of the greedy. Causing us to
not believe, even though we are so needy.
I am finding solutions to help me, when I leave here. So,
I thank you for your assistance in helping me to be me.

Hank

"There is a light at the end of the tunnel. Just because you're down doesn't mean that you're going to be down forever."

Christmas has to be my favorite time of the year. My birthday is around that time. It was great because I got a lot of Christmas presents at once. It was like, "Oh my God, presents everywhere!" I remember that my grandmother would literally make me go to sleep. I wanted to stay up and see Santa. She would tell me that Santa would not come if the kids are not asleep. Those were some of my best memories, Christmas.

It was also hard for me. I grew up in a small town in the South. My mother was Caucasian and my dad was African American. I was also an only child, and growing up with a physical disability, club foot, made it more difficult. It left me in a wheelchair. I'll talk more about that later. It didn't help that my mom was a heroin addict and my father was an alcoholic. I really do not remember them much because they divorced before I could remember.

The toughest part of my childhood was pronouncing my *papa* dead. I was eight years old when that happened. My grandfather and I were more like brothers than grandson and grandpa. I went to wake him up and he did not want to wake up. I got my grandmother and she attempted without any luck either. She got on the phone and called my uncles who did not live far down the road. But before they arrived, I knew. I knew he was not breathing and had to pronounce him dead. I blamed God for a long time. After my grandfather died, my grandmother could not handle me. I had a lot of hyper-activeness, which would cause me to get up and go burn off, without telling anyone where I was going. With these episodes it was difficult for her to care for me and because of this, she decided to put me in my first group home at the age of eight.

It was hard growing up. My mom was a drug addict on heroin. She used to make me drink from the toilet. The last time I spoke to my mother, I kicked her and her boyfriend out of my house. I received a call one day to my house when I was younger. I answered and a woman asked to speak to Hank. I said, "This is Hank." "No, Hank, senior," she replied. I passed the phone. When I got it back, she said, "This is your mother." My mouth dropped in awe. I even dropped the phone. I didn't know how to respond. She mentioned I had a sister, but she didn't know her name or anything about her. All she wanted was for me to pick her up. So I went. She was with this other white dude. He kept on using the "N" word all the way home. Eventually I got fed up with it. When we got to my house I told him, "You've got one more time to say the 'N' word before I show you what the 'N' word *is*." He said it again. I beat that man so bad. Then I turned around to my mother and I told her, "You can go, too. You brought this trash to my house, you can leave with it." That was the last time I saw her. Last I heard she was doing life in prison, but I cannot seem to find her.

The group home was located in a town in the South. A group home is where a bunch of kids live together, attend school, and all kinds of stuff. I had to share a room with three to four other members, which was one thing I disliked about the group home. During Christmas time, the group home would drive us to visit our family. I looked forward to these trips. I remained at the group home until I was about sixteen to seventeen years old. I started to make bad choices, and in my twenties I became homeless for the first time. I allowed people to stay with me that I shouldn't have, and different things.

Being homeless was really scary because I didn't know what to expect. I was a nervous wreck. I learned through my homeless experience to look out for myself and not to trust everybody. This was difficult for me because I'm the type of person that will give my shirt off my back if you need it. I ran into a couple of occasions where I had a knife pulled on me. I've been jumped, but it wasn't nothing I couldn't handle. I pretty much raised myself. Everything I know is street smarts, knowledge on how to survive. I was pretty much raised on the streets.

About 5 years ago I was involved with a group home and I began mixing in with the wrong crowd. One night I went with them to do an aggravated robbery. I was left in the car with the weapons. I was arrested and charged with aggravated robbery and was in jail for about five years. I was facing five to ninety-nine years if it went to trial. My lawyer said it was best to submit a plea. I served the sentence. I could have gotten out on good behavior, but I was in the state of mind where I didn't answer to anybody. I didn't even answer to my parents. I know that is bad because they brought me into this world. The jail attempted to rehabilitate me, but with my disability it was difficult.

It became difficult because not a lot of people understand what it means to have a disability, much less a mental one. It pisses me off because there would be people walking down the streets and I began to question it. "What the hell are you looking at?" "Take a picture!" I managed with time, however, to just let it roll off my shoulders. I just thought, maybe they have a bigger problem than I do. It was still difficult nonetheless.

I went back to being homeless after I got out of jail. I used to work for a company, but it shut down while I was in jail. I had nowhere to go, but to a homeless shelter. I have been with the program at the shelter for about four to six months now. They will help me stabilize with apartment assistance for a year. If I could tell people something about being homeless, it would be: keep your head up, help yourself, and utilize your resources. There is light at the end of the tunnel – just because you are down, doesn't mean that you are going to be down forever. We need to help ourselves from becoming homeless in any way that we can. If it does happen, use your resources. If you have a drug problem and you're at a shelter, check yourself into rehab.

I have aspirations. I have a fiancée. We have been together since 2002. She is the apple of my eye. She supported me when I was incarcerated and I am hoping to move to where she is at so that way we can actually be together. I would like to get to know my sister. Family is very important to me. She has a brother, which is me, and she doesn't know anything about him. I would like to get into my own apartment – maybe get some help. There are certain things I can and cannot do because of my disability. Being diagnosed with Bipolar, Schizophrenia, and experiencing suicidal ideations has been a lot to handle. Just because I am disabled does not mean that I am different than everybody else. It just means that I have a problem. I need to push forward. My dream is to own an expensive sports car. A blue or light blue one. A lot of people say, "Oh look at him, he's homeless," but we have free access to soap and water. I stay clean. It is not my choice that I am homeless. If I could have avoided it I would have.

By Christy

Roy

━━━━━━━━━━━━━━━━━━━━━━

"I might be working at a car wash in the winter time, but a job is a job is a job."

I woke up in the hospital and they were pulling the catheter out of me and my leg was bleeding from the IV. I sat up when I saw this and they put me back down and pulled the tube out of my throat. I had been on a ventilator for two days in an induced coma. I was found on the side of the road barely breathing. I have had two incidents here where I have blacked out and fallen down. I have seizure disorder and this isn't the first time this kind of incidence has occurred. I have what's called a "walking seizure." For example, I'm not even driving and my body goes on. I've had one experience where I was walking and functioning, and I had no control over what I was doing, but my body did exactly what I should be doing at that time which kind of amazed me. When I saw people they talked to me, but I didn't speak back to them. I just went through my daily routine, got my medication and wrote down my name walked off and went out the back door and that's when I got control over myself and that was scary!

I was 11 years old when my father got me a rare dirt bike. This was when I got into racing. My last motorcycle was a rocket. It was the fastest bike I had ever ridden. The last thing I remember about that bike is grabbing my helmet and saying I'm going for a ride. Next thing I know, it's three days later I was getting my back door kicked in and I sat up in the bed. I yelled in pain, "My back, my back!" My girlfriend was there, I looked at her and said, "What happened?"

She said, "You crashed your bike." My hair was still matted and dried with blood. I guess I had been laying there in a coma for three days. I wasn't supposed to go to sleep, but I have no memory of any accident; I have no memory of anything. I had lost my memory; luckily I knew people's names and my name. Took me a while to get my memory back. But every memory I had to see all over again. I just didn't think later about something and there it was. It got rerouted through my brain and I had to see everything as it got rerouted. For example, I was able to call my ex-wife's phone number from memory, now it's a number I had forgotten. Turns out I damaged my frontal lobe of my brain, and I went into a corner at ninety miles an hour and they had changed the road because it had washed out and I hit a rock as big as a car and flew 134 feet before I hit the ground. Didn't even scratch the helmet, but it was filled with blood. The hospital threw me out and said I was too combative, that's a sign of a head injury.

After being thrown out, Laura took me to her father, and her brother went to pick my motorcycle up out of the canyon. That was the beginning of my downfall because my kind nature started to go downhill from then and I kept picking up assault charges, battery charges, just violent charges. It wasn't until 1999 and this anger management class was available and I took it and it really helped a lot, really helped a lot. It turns out that the damage in my brain controls my emotions and my cognitive reasoning, and it's the same thing as having a frontal lobotomy because it's located in that area. I can't control or regulate anything. This is going to sound weird, but ever since Laura, my first wife, I've never fallen in love with another woman. I can feel love or lust, but I have never fallen in love with another woman. It's been some time now, 24 years.

I got my third DUI and when my attorney looked at my record and said, "You don't have a record until 1991. What happened?" I told him about the accident and he said, "Yeah, I noticed you're not normal," and sent me to a neuropsychologist. She did a 2 day service study on me, and my new wife, who I just married, read the report and said she wanted a divorce.

She got her divorce at her expense. I started living with my sister because I just got out of prison and now I'm on parole. I was going online looking for jobs, and I got a resume built. Doing lawn work with this guy and drinking my money away is how I spent my time. My garage was set up as a man's cave. I loved the stereo I had in there and I loved the fact that every tool I owned was in there too. Time went on and I even had my son out there and he got sent back by my sister – that killed me. My daughter and I still keep in contact. I have 2 children, a boy and a girl, by two different mothers. They both live in different in a different state than me. One has bone cancer and leukemia right now. They want to remove half of her liver, but they can't operate on her right now because she is too weak. She won't talk to me. All over a freaking computer that I was pissed off about because she wouldn't give it back. I said some real, real cruel words and I don't doubt that she will ever talk to me again. I texted my daughter's mother, Sara, "Please let me make contact with my daughter." She said okay, but I haven't heard anything. I'm not trying to push the issue because I can push her away and make it worse. So I just have to deal with it one day at a time.

Back to living with my sister, it's going nowhere and having nothing was really getting to me. I guess you can say my depression grew and my anxieties got worse. Every day it was something different and I couldn't deal with it, couldn't deal with it. I had been searching and searching for a place to go, to a place to move to. I don't know why, but I picked up my phone and made a call to a crisis intervention line. I was ranting and raving and I told her I just want to pop a bullet in my head. Next thing I know the police were there and I'm going to a hospital. I ended up in a crisis stabilization unit locked up and being evaluated. First time in my life I get a diagnosis of bipolar manic depression schizophrenic, go figure.

That experience explained a lot to me and opened my eyes. I thought everyone heard voices. It comes to me that I've always put a song in my mind or something trying to distract myself whenever I'm doing anything. I've always got three things going at the same time. I'm here talking to you and thinking of something else and spinning this thing in my hand. There are no voices right now, which is a good thing. I was told not to be isolated because that's when it's worse. Keep your mind occupied if you don't use it you'll lose it.

The crisis stabilization unit kept me for a while and they gave me a diagnosis and then they put me out, and I went looking for a job the first day. I got kicked out because I'm not supposed to leave for 90 days, so I went and got drunk. Then I'm in the town, not a dime in my pocket. I go to a mental health rehabilitation clinic and I figured they would let me back in. They gave me a bus ticket to a large city nearby, there's this beautiful shelter there they tell me, and I came here and got stuck sleeping outside. I couldn't believe what I saw. I met people there and some of them were on disability and they want to be there, and some are on disability and they don't want to be there. Some people don't want to be there period and want to move on and some people that is just the way their life is and they love it.

Me, I didn't like it one bit. I wanted out of there and I found an old man named Frank and we'd go and sit and drink our beers out wherever we could. We were sitting outside one day drinking our 40s and up pulled this white car. This woman says, "Can you cook and clean? Can you cook for people and clean a house?" I said, "Hell yes, I can," and she said, "Do you want a job?" She asked Frank if he collects disability and asked, "Do you want to go to a boarding house?" He said yes.

So I land a job and he lands a place to live. So I'm a house manager now, no background no nothing she doesn't even ask if I have a drug problem. I'm an alcoholic.

I dispense medications and keep track of everything, I do all the cooking, I do all the cleaning, and I do the yard work. I take care of up to eight people at one time. It's free room and board, I just have to use my food stamps. She does that to everybody, she rips them off. That lasted for a couple of months. Me and her always had our falling outs. One guy kept calling the police, kept calling the police and the police said if I get called one more time you're both going to jail. He called the police again and I just said let's just give them a reason to take us and I punched him. The fight was on and the police came in and we were fighting, we both went to jail. I got time served and he got six months of probation, anger management and community service. But I'm back to sleeping outside again. There are some people there that are honest and just want to make it. You have to find the right people and you have to set pacts with them so somebody pretty much stands guard over your goods. You can't leave anything anywhere you can't even sleep with anything out or it's stolen. I understand what they are trying to do over there, but there is so much trash for people in there and that's their way of life, they don't want to move up.

I ended up going to the program at the shelter. My caseworker asked me how long I had been drinking and said don't you think it's time that you get sober and go to detox, and I said yes. Her name was Julie; God had sent me an angel that day. I went to detox and from there I went to the program and I walked the steps and I actually got nine months sober. I moved to the member side after three months, got my own single room, and started on the job training. Landed a job a real job working as a bus boy, I wasn't picky but that lasted a week. My sciatic blew out I couldn't do the job so there went that job. I have disability pending; not only do I have seizure disorder, but I have degenerative joint disease of my spine all the way down to my tail bone and my sciatic is a big problem. My disability is pending and ever since the incident in the hospital when I woke up with a respirator they said I have COPD (Chronic Obstructive Pulmonary Disease) and disability called me and they want to know what the doctor's opinion is when I go to the pulmonary doctor on the 9th of this month and my PCP on the 10th. So that's going to be the determination of the disability.

In the future, I'm hoping to go see my father. My sister wants to drive out there because it's the cheapest way. She works for the government, but they're doing their cut backs. She had to sell her house and it's ugly. Hopefully, we can stop on the way back so I can see my daughter and surprise her. Hug her and say I'm sorry. My plans for the future are a big fear right now. I don't have a job. I'm a three time felon because of two DUIs and one threatening an officer. I'm a three time felon for stupid shit. It's called alcohol, my friend. Getting a place to live and getting a job is hard enough now my credit is destroyed and I'm a felon. So that's going to be near impossible. I have three months to have all this shit together. I might be working at a car wash in the winter time, but a job is a job is a job.

Homelessness can happen to anyone. Some people it's a choice to them. My past girlfriend was homeless for 10 years and that was by choice. Now that she has been saved and is moving on she's got a condescending attitude and all I want to tell her is remember who was out there by choice. I wasn't out there by choice, but I was out there. I was taking that crappy job as house manager, this year alone I took that job for five months. It's a hell of a job – everyone there is handicapped and mentally challenged, and it's a 24/7 job. Those people that she has in that home were homeless. They might have been receiving checks, but a lot of them some of them didn't know how to get out of being homeless. How they became homeless, I don't know. I became homeless in my own way. I lost everything when I went to prison, I trusted my wife, I lost everything I had nothing when I came out. I trusted in my sister and she gave me everything she could, but I still fell apart. Right now I'm a 50 year old man and look what I have. I have a mountain bike and I live out of a locker. A job and security is all I ask for. Isn't that a dream? That's my hope is to get a job that's secure that way I can get a place to live and have some security and save some money, get stuck with the bills get stuck with payments actually move up and actually be able to buy a house even at my age. Either that or live in a motel, I don't know. It's hard to think that far ahead. I've been trying to get a real job for so long and you get these emails back, "We appreciate you at this time but you don't meet our qualifications." I know what they did, they checked my background or my credit score, but one hotel still emails me about job openings and you know how many times I've gone in and listed for that opening. I've got how many weeks of janitorial training here, man they won't hire me. There is one part I forgot to mention is this seizure disorder that I have is brought on by the brain damage and it was about a year after the accident when I had my first grand mal seizure and they looked at my head and they found that there's a big scar on my frontal lobe and that would explain why I always had blood coming out of my eye and nose bleeds all the time. I'm just thankful that they have been diagnosing people at a young age so they don't have to go through life like I did, just back and forth, two different people. That's what everyone said to me all my life you're like two different people, well guess what? That's me.

By John

Epilogue

The first-hand experiences gained through this class project serve as the basis for the following recommendations:

1. Individuals experiencing homelessness need to be treated with dignity and respect regardless of their condition. Their stories and needs reflect their diversity, suggesting that policies and programs that support them also need to be diverse.
2. There is a pressing need for better services for persons who are homeless and are experiencing co-occurring mental health and substance use problems. Many individuals who are homeless have histories that include serious trauma and loss. Services need to incorporate assessment and intervention that focus on these issues when appropriate.
3. A better job of educating the public about the life outcomes of persons with mental illness is needed,

especially for homeless persons experiencing mental health issues.

4. Policy makers need to pay more attention to creating legislation (and the funding required to carry out that legislation) that supports positive mental health outcomes for all members of society;

5. "Housing first" or "rapid re-housing" initiatives for persons experiencing homelessness must be coupled with wrap-around support services (for example, case management, information and referral to needed resources, counseling, help in finding and keeping jobs, parenting education, nutrition classes, health care, medication) in order to reduce the cycle of homelessness, particularly for those with co-occurring mental health and substance use disorders.

6. Incarceration of homeless individuals with mental health problems needs to end. Prison is no substitute for community-based care for individuals with severe and persistent mental health problems.

7. The "quick fix" approach that has characterized programs and services for homeless individuals with mental health and substance use disorders needs to be replaced with one that embraces a long-term view of addressing the problem. Some individuals can function well with medication and social support, but they may never be able to be completely self-sufficient (without any type of financial or other assistance).

8. City planners and advocates for the homeless should work together to develop creative housing alternatives

that prevent people from becoming homeless and allow persons experiencing homelessness to secure permanent housing.

9. The media in all its forms need to present an accurate and balanced picture of what it is like to be homeless in America, especially for those with mental health and substance use disorders.

10. An assets-based approach to community building is needed to adequately address the antecedents and consequences of homelessness.

All of the men and women whose stories appear in this book have hopes and dreams for a better future. Some are simple, like having holiday gatherings with family members. Others are more ambitious, like obtaining a college degree. Whether these hopes and dreams will be realized is difficult to predict. The sheer fact that they exist at all is compelling testimony to their strength, resilience, and will to survive demonstrated by the men and women whose stories appear here. They are still standing in spite of the horrific things they experienced. It is our wish that their hopes and dreams are fulfilled.